MY GOD

SELECTED PSALMS

KEN FLEMING

Developed as a study course by Emmaus Correspondence School, founded in 1942.

My God and I: Selected Psalms

Ken Fleming

Published by:

Emmaus Correspondence School
(A division of ECS Ministries)
P.O. Box 1028
Dubuque, IA 52004-1028
phone: (563) 585-2070
email: ecsorders@ecsministries.org
website: www.ecsministries.org

First Printing 2009 (AK '09), 2 Units

ISBN 978-1-59387-105-5

Printed in the United States of America

STUDENT INSTRUCTIONS

Lessons You Will Study

Course Components

This course has two parts: this study course and the exam booklet.

How To Study

This study has twelve chapters, and each chapter has its own exam. Begin by asking God to help you understand the material. Read the chapter through at least twice, once to get a general idea of its contents and then again, slowly, looking up any Bible references given.

Begin studying immediately, or if you are in a group, as soon as the group begins. We suggest that you keep a regular schedule by trying to complete at least one chapter per week.

Exams

In the exam booklet there is one exam for each chapter (exam 1 covers chapter 1 of the course). Do not answer the questions by what you think or have always believed. The questions are designed to find out if you understand the material given in the course.

After you have completed each chapter, review the related exam and see how well you know the answers. If you find that you are having difficulty answering the questions, review the material until you think you can answer the questions.

How Your Exams Are Graded

Your instructor will mark any incorrectly answered questions. You will be referred back to the place in the course where the correct answer is to be found. After finishing this course with a passing average, you will be awarded a certificate.

If you enrolled in a class, submit your exam papers to the leader or secretary of the class who will send them for the entire group to the Correspondence School.

See the back of the exam booklet for more information on returning the exams for grading.

INTRODUCTION

The book of Psalms, a collection of 150 Hebrew poems, has been the devotional favorite of God's people down through the centuries. In the Psalms, believers in times past expressed their hearts to God. And even though their circumstances differed so much from ours today, we can readily identify with their writings because they express man's inmost feelings.

When we are discouraged, the Psalms lift our spirits. When we think God is distant, they help us sense that He is, in fact, near. When we are sad, they remind us of God's steadfast love, providing a sense of perspective. When we are happy, they give us words to express our praise to God. When tragedy strikes, they give comfort. When we feel lonely, they remind us of God's never-failing presence. In our doubts we find reason to exercise faith, and in our weakness we find strength to endure our hardships. When those around us are unfaithful, we discover that God is ever-faithful. When we are unjustly treated, we echo the cries of these Old Testament saints who yearned for justice and vindication. No wonder Psalms is such a well-loved book of the Bible!

The word *psalm* means "praise," and the content of many of them reflect this. David is the author of approximately half of them, with six other authors mentioned, chiefly Asaph and Korah. Fifty are anonymous. Most of them were written as lyrics to be accompanied by the lyre, a favorite musical instrument of those times. The Israelites would have probably sung them in connection with regular worship in the temple and when groups of pilgrims traveled to the annual feasts.

Much of the poetry is written in pairs of lines that are related to each other. In some pairs the second line expresses the same thought as the first, but in different words:

> *"Hear my prayer, O Lord,*
> *And let my cry come to You"* (102:1).

In others, the second line contrasts with the first line:

> *"For the Lord knows the way of the righteous,*
> *But the way of the ungodly shall perish"* (1:6).

And in still in others the second line adds something to what is stated in the first:

> *"For who is God, except the Lord,*
> *And who is a rock, except our God?"* (18:31)

When you observe this parallel structure, it will not only add to your enjoyment of them but will caution you to take into account the fact that, as poetry, they are not to be interpreted in the same way that doctrinal (or even narrative) passages are interpreted. The Psalms *are* part of the inspired Scriptures, but they are written from man's perspective; they are valuable in that they do speak to and for our hearts, but we should not base doctrine on them without support from other portions of the Bible. It is also important to remember that the Old Testament should be interpreted in light of what God has revealed to us in the New Testament. For example, as New Testament Christians who are indwelt permanently by the Holy Spirit, we do not need to pray as David did when he sinned, "Do not take Your Holy Spirit from me" (51:11).

The psalms selected for this ECS study course cover the believer's response to God amid the circumstances of life. In this selection, the writers relate some aspect of God's person to their particular situation. May your study of these psalms open your eyes to the character of God in relation to your own heart and life.

1

PSALM 1
THE LORD IS MY GOD

O ne of the underlying themes of the whole book of Psalms is the wisdom of choosing to belong to God and following Him as opposed to the foolishness of rejecting God and following the way of the world and ungodliness. Psalm 1 is a gateway to all the other psalms in that it sets the tone for them all. It describes two kinds of people—the "righteous" and the "ungodly"—and proclaims the fact that God blesses the righteous and condemns the ungodly.

> *Psalm 1 is a gateway to all the other psalms.*

The Righteous and the Ungodly Contrasted

"Righteous" people may be defined biblically in two ways. They are those who are *righteous by position;* they have been counted righteous (justified) in God's sight because they have exercised faith in God to save them (Gen. 15:6; Rom. 1:17). They are also *righteous in practice*—that is, they practice their faith in God, seeking to please Him by the way they live. The "ungodly" constitute the vast majority of mankind. They are not only born "dead in trespasses and sins" and therefore "condemned already" (Eph. 2:1; John 3:18); they also sin actively in attitude, word, and deed (Rom. 3:10-18).

The psalm describes in broad terms the mindset, priorities, and destiny of the righteous person in contrast to the mindset, priorities, and destiny of the ungodly. Verses 1-3 relate to the godly; verses 4-5 to the ungodly; and verse 6 relates to both. Psalm 1 can be classified as a "wisdom" psalm because it calls on those who would be wise to choose to follow God's teachings that we find in the Bible. It can be compared to other wisdom literature in the Bible where there is a right way to be chosen and a wrong way to be avoided, and even the righteous must make choices.

Psalm 1 asserts in brief that the good and godly life will result in maximum spiritual enjoyment and blessing. It is blessing that far exceeds what the world offers, with its pleasures, possessions, and positions of honor and power. This blessing comprises the greater enjoyment of knowing God and obeying Him. It is clear that the anonymous author of this psalm experienced firsthand "the good life" that God offers and wanted others to know its value. He puts the lie to the notion that what the world calls the good life is really good—it will turn out instead not only to be empty, but to lead to judgment.

> Godly life will result in maximum spiritual enjoyment and blessing.

The Righteous are "Blessed"

Psalm 1 begins with a beatitude, or blessing. The psalmist is stating a fact. The word "blessed" occurs more times in the book of Psalms than in all the other books of the Bible put together. Blessedness is the supreme condition of the godly person. It is actually a plural noun in the original language and could be read as "O, the blessednesses," referring to the multiplied joys that God desires to pour out on His people. God designed mankind to be blessed. In the beginning, when God created Adam and Eve in His own image, the first thing He did was to bless them (Gen. 1:27-28). If you want to be a genuinely happy man or woman, Psalm 1 provides a key to being so.

Keep in mind that blessedness is not an arbitrary bestowment by God on certain privileged people. It does not depend on the pleasantness of surroundings or circumstances. Nor is it measured in how many possessions one has. The blessing we experience results from how we deal with two key relationships: our relationship with God and our relationship with the world. Blessedness is not an elusive dream. It is available for all who choose to heed what God says about these two relationships.

The Way of the Godly (vv. 1-3)

The Righteous Reject the World (v. 1)

Blessed is the man or woman who chooses not to conform to the lifestyle of this ungodly world. This is the biblical principle of separation. Verse 1 does not imply that godly believers should have no contact with ungodly people. We are to live in the world and should influence it for good. We are to be light in a dark world, salt in a corrupt world, and righteous in a wicked world. The Lord Jesus Christ acknowledged that His disciples would live *in* the world but prayed that God's truth in His Word would be the means of their not being *of* the world (John 17:16-18). The psalmist begins by stating that the righteous person is one who actively refuses to be *of* the world and that this stance would result in his being blessed of God.

In three phrases he characterizes the godly person as one who rejects the value systems of the world in which he lives. In Hebrew poetry there are often parallel lines that are poetically synonymous. That is, each line states the same general theme. Notice the parallels in these three lines: "Blessed is the man who walks not in the counsel of the ungodly, nor stands in the path of sinners, nor sits in the seat of the scornful."

The lifestyle of the world is to be avoided.

In practicing separation, there are three things the godly person does not do, three spheres he does not frequent, and three different descriptions of the worldly people he avoids. As we unwrap these three phrases we must keep in mind the central principle, which is that the lifestyle of the world is to be avoided. Because this is Hebrew poetry, we are not meant to view these descriptions as distinct theological truths.

"Who walks not in the counsel of the ungodly"

When we choose not to walk in the counsel of the ungodly, the result will be that we will not be shaped by their worldly advice. The ungodly cannot give good counsel to a believer because they leave God out of their reckoning. They reject divine authority and biblical wisdom and can know nothing of heavenly wisdom (cf. James 3:15-17). They never take into account God's righteousness or His glory. When we refuse to "walk" or "go" in the direction the ungodly go, we will not be impressed or affected by the philosophies that govern *their* lives.

"nor stands in the path of sinners"

To choose to not stand in the way of sinners is to refuse to associate with them in their sinful lifestyle. The "path of sinners" describes their manner of life and is in contrast to the "way of the righteous" in verse 6. We are not to associate with their corrupt practices, because they do not represent God's righteous standards. Here, the example of Samson is helpful. Samson was born to be a Nazarite (Judges 13:7). A Nazarite was one who consecrated himself to live for God and serve Him. But Samson preferred the lifestyle of the Philistines, particularly their flagrant sensuality, and he never knew the blessedness God had for him (read Judges chapters 14-16 for the full story).

"nor sits in the seat of the scornful"

To not sit in the seat of the scornful is to not participate with the ungodly when they scorn the holy things of God. The word "seat" may also be translated "assembly." When the ungodly get together, they mock the biblical norms of absolute truth, sexual morality, and ethical standards. Lot's life illustrates this clearly. He joined the assembly of the wicked city elders of Sodom even though their mocking vexed his righteous soul (2 Peter 2:7-8). His close association with them had a devastating effect on his family (Genesis 19).

Psalm 1:1 describes the downward progression of the influence of the wicked. The first step downward is to listen to their counsel. The next step is to willfully break God's commandments. The final step is to join the assembly of the mockers and heap scorn on those who practice God's standards of righteousness. Blessed is the believer who refuses to be molded by the world. It starts with bad advice; it continues with sinful actions; and it reaches a climax when we hold what is holy in contempt. We are exhorted in the New Testament, "Do not be conformed to this world," and "Come out from among them and be separate" (Rom. 12:2; 2 Cor. 6:17).

The Righteous Esteem God's Word (v. 2)

We have learned that the righteous man is one whose relationship with the world is one of rejection and opposition. The other key relationship of the righteous man is his relationship with God and His Word, which is one of enjoyment and submission. We will call this the principle of devotion. The righteous man is described as one whose "delight is in the law of the Lord."

God's "law" does not refer only to the legal sections of the first five books of the Bible. It is a common synonym for the whole Word of God (Josh. 1:7). It is the *Torah* in Hebrew, which means "instruction from God."

To delight in God's law is to want to learn about God and His instruction to us. God's law reflects His holy character. To delight in the law is to have an insatiable hunger to know more of God and His will and to actually do it. Delighting in God's ways is a primary indication of spiritual life in contrast to the worldly mind that is hostile to God and does not submit to His law (Rom. 8:7). We should identify with the psalmist in Psalm 119:97 who wrote, "Oh, how I love Your law!"

> ──── ❧ ────
> **The key relationship of the righteous man is his relationship with God and His Word.**
> ──── ❧ ────

The one who delights in God's law will meditate on it day and night. That does not mean that he never thinks of anything else, but it does mean that he applies the principles of the Word to everything he does or says. We all meditate on those things we are passionate about. It may be sports, clothes, cars, work, or a host of other things. What we "love" is what we think about. When we have a passion for God's Word, we will continually go over the text in our minds and consider its implications with the result that the indwelling Spirit of God will be free to apply it to different aspects of our daily life.

The word *meditate* means to "ponder by talking to oneself." Biblical meditation is the purposeful engaging of the conscious mind on the Word toward greater understanding and application. There are sins to avoid, promises to claim, victories to win, and praises to be expressed. Biblical meditation is a discipline of the mind to consider Scripture and to be able to verbalize what you learn. The degree to which we can put our thoughts into words on *any* topic is the measure of what we have truly learned and absorbed about that topic. To practice biblical meditation will mean turning off the TV, music, cell phone, and computer—in short, any visible or audible distractions.

The Righteous Bear Spiritual Fruit (v. 3)

In verses 1 and 2 the psalmist has described the righteous man in two ways: first, as one who rejects the ungodly world; second, as the one who embraces the law of the Lord. We now see that *separation* from the world (a negative attitude) and *devotion* to the Lord (a positive attitude) results in spiritual *fruition*. God, the Planter, carefully places the righteous person where he or she can bear the fruit that He desires. In that place there will be "rivers," or literally "irrigation channels," of "water." Irrigation channels indicate that God not only places the tree but provides water for it. Although times of drought may come, there will always be a supply of life-giving spiritual refreshment so His servant can give evidence of his relationship to the Lord.

The water in the soil dissolves the nutrients. Those moistened nutrients are absorbed by the tree, which spreads out its roots to reach them (cf. Jeremiah 17:8, where the same imagery is used). The nutrients are absorbed by the roots and transported unseen up through the trunk to its branches and leaves. Eventually they form the flowers and the fruit. It is a wonderful picture of the unseen work of the Spirit of God in us to produce spiritual fruit in our lives. Jeremiah 17:8 adds the detail that the tree "spreads out its roots by the river." The importance of the supply of water to the tree, so it can bear fruit, cannot be overstated.

The properly planted tree, deeply rooted in the Word of God and well watered by the Spirit of God, should do more than just stand there; it should bear fruit. In biblical terms, fruit manifests itself in a number of ways, but we'll just mention here some Christ-like characteristics that the righteous person will demonstrate when he or she is yielded to the Holy Spirit's control: love, joy, peace, longsuffering, kindness, goodness, faithfulness, gentleness, and self control. These are called the fruit of the Spirit (Gal. 5:22). They appear best when there is continuous inner renewal in our souls. They have nothing to do with what we call "success" and everything to do with godly character.

Another feature of the tree by the channels of water is that its leaf does not wither, a picture of steadfastness and continual testimony of the fact that the tree is alive and healthy. The leaves are not only a means of sustaining life but they beautify the tree and do not wither, even in drought.

The final phrase of verse 3 says, "And whatsoever he does shall prosper." The prosperity of the righteous man is measured by the God-honoring spiritual prosperity that becomes evident in his family life, his church life, and his working life. Jesus said to His disciples, "By this My Father is glorified, that you bear much fruit" (John 15:8).

The Way of the Ungodly (vv. 4-5)

The second illustration taken from the agriculture of ancient Israel is about the ungodly, who are contrasted to the godly by the phrase, "The ungodly are not so." The Septuagint (the Greek translation of the Hebrew Old Testament) states it with a double negative: "Not so, the ungodly, not so." They are like the chaff on a threshing floor, which is separated from the kernels of ripe grain by animals tramping on it or by men beating it with implements. Threshing floors were placed on hilltops, where it was windy. The separated chaff and grain were thrown into the wind with shovels. The grain, being heavier, would fall back on the floor, while the chaff would be blown away by the wind. This pictures the end of the empty, worthless life of the ungodly in contrast to the fruit-bearing prosperity of the godly.

Threshing and separating the wheat from the husks is a common biblical description for the destruction and judgment of the ungodly. John the Baptist used this imagery when he said that the coming Messiah would "thoroughly clean out His threshing floor, and gather the wheat into His barn; but the chaff He will burn with unquenchable fire" (Luke 3:17). The tree of the righteous will stand unaffected by the storm of judgment, but the chaff will be blown or driven away (cf. Job 21:18). The ungodly person is *not* the master of his own fate; rather, he is being relentlessly driven by the winds of God's judgment.

The psalmist clearly indicates the fate of the ungodly by the word "therefore." The ungodly cannot "stand" before the judge, because they are guilty (2 Thess. 1:8-9). They will therefore suffer eternal destruction. The psalmist may have been implying judgment in the sense of ongoing judgment in the lives of the wicked, but there are overtones of eternal judgment here. Certainly the ungodly will not enjoy the "congregation of the righteous" in heaven, but will be forever excluded.

Words of Comfort, Words of Warning (v. 6)

The psalm concludes, "For the Lord knows the way of the righteous" (v. 6). God knows and understands that living in this fallen world is difficult for those who have chosen to please Him and to put the world behind them. He is very much aware that we are constantly opposed by the ungodly. God knows all Satan's wiles, how he constantly seeks to trip up God's people. The psalmist reminds us that the way of the ungodly will end in destruction, in contrast to the path of the godly that leads to eternal blessing.

The Word of God is clear that every human being will spend eternity in one of two places—either with God or excluded from His presence in the lake of fire (Rev. 21:15). That conclusion is legitimately seen in Psalm 1. But it is also true that, as a wisdom psalm, it contains an underlying message of warning for believers to make right choices every day regarding our relationships with both God and the world around us. In so doing we can truly experience the spiritual blessedness God intends for those who are righteous in practice as well as by position. And while enjoying this blessedness, we will be a source of blessing to those around us.

2

PSALM 23
THE LORD IS MY CARING SHEPHERD

For 3000 years the twenty-third psalm has inspired, comforted, and encouraged God's people. Maybe one reason for this is that it is intensely personal, using the personal pronouns "I," "me," and "my" seventeen times in its six verses.

Placed where it is in the whole book of Psalms, Psalm 23 is the second of three psalms that uniquely foreshadow the Lord Jesus Christ. Psalm 22 foreshadows Him dying for us as our Savior; Psalm 23 foreshadows Him in His High Priestly ministry in heaven, caring for us as our Shepherd; and Psalm 24 foreshadows Him on His throne, reigning over us as our Sovereign. Psalm 23 is the song of the once-lost sheep that has been found by the Shepherd and is now safely in His care. We believers are those lost and wandering sheep (Isa. 53:6). But our Shepherd loved us and came to rescue us. We are now His people and the sheep of His pasture (Ps. 100:3). And from the security of the flock we can sing this song with David.

Historical Background

As a boy, long before he became king, David had worked as a shepherd (1 Sam. 16:1; 11-13). We can picture him in the pasturelands around Bethlehem surrounded by his father's flock, his sheep grazing contentedly. He has protected them from wild animals, brought back the strays, and dressed the wounded. His sheep have come to trust him and then to rest contentedly. Maybe, as David began thinking about how his relationship with his sheep reflected the relationship between God and His people (and particularly himself), he penned this song.

"The Lord is my shepherd" (v. 1)

The first word of the psalm is "The LORD," or Yahweh. This name was revealed to Moses at the burning bush in the desert of Sinai as the "I AM," the timeless, changeless, all-sufficient God who faithfully keeps His promises (Exodus 3). Now David confesses Yahweh as his own personal Shepherd.

"The LORD is my shepherd" is the signature line of the whole psalm. Abraham, Isaac, and Jacob had all been shepherds, and their descendants continued as such in Egypt as well as when the Israelite nation settled back in Canaan. It is no wonder that the metaphor of a shepherd and his sheep is used frequently in the Psalms and the prophetic writings, as it describes so well the relationship between God and His people (see Psalms 77:20, 78:52, 79:13, and 100:3; Isaiah 40:11; Jeremiah 31:10; and Ezekiel 34:11-16).

> Jesus Christ is our Shepherd—past, present, and future.

In the New Testament we learn that the Lord Jesus Christ is the Shepherd of those who have placed their trust in Him to save them from eternal punishment for their sins (1 Peter 2:24-25). In John's gospel Jesus reveals Himself as *the good shepherd* who would soon give His life for His sheep (John 10:11). In Hebrews 13:20-21 we read that He is *that great Shepherd* who rose from the dead and provides for His sheep so they can serve Him. And Peter calls Christ *the Chief Shepherd* who will reward His under-shepherds (overseers of local churches) when He comes again (1 Peter 5:4). Thus, Jesus Christ is our Shepherd—past, present, and future. Those who believe in Him can confidently say with David, "The LORD is my shepherd."

Notice that David calls God "*my* shepherd." The LORD is not only *the* Shepherd of *the* flock; He is *my* Shepherd. A young boy was dying of cancer. His mother taught him Psalm 23 by having him repeat "The LORD is my shepherd" while counting on his five fingers, starting with his thumb. She showed him how to hold his finger when he got to the word, "my." When he died a few days later, the boy was found with his little fist wrapped around the ring finger of his other hand.

As a result of Yahweh being my Shepherd, I can confidently say, "I shall not want"; in other words, I will never lack anything I need. David the shepherd boy knew well that his sheep needed him for every aspect of their welfare. In his relationship with the Lord as his Shepherd, David was the sheep, and he knew that he would never lack anything necessary for his own well-being. We can have that same assurance if we are one of God's sheep.

In the next four verses, David records eight important needs that have been fully met by his Shepherd.

1. The Shepherd Gives Rest (v. 2)

The image here is of the sheep lying down in lush pasture. They are resting contentedly. Sheep do not often relax and lie down in the sun as cows do. Phillip Keller, the Christian shepherd and author of *A Shepherd Looks at Psalm 23*, says that sheep will hardly lie down unless four requirements are met: (1) they must be free from the fear of danger; (2) they must be free from social friction in the flock (often caused by dominant rams); (3) they must be free from the irritation of insects like flies and ticks; and (4) they must be free from hunger.

The shepherd would choose a meadow for its green grass to feed them, its safety, and its suitability for the sheep. His provision and his presence would enable them to feel at ease enough to lie down to rest. Jesus our Shepherd also provides rest for His sheep. He promises that those who come to Him will find rest for their souls (Matt. 11:28-29), which in that context was freedom from striving to keep the law as a means of becoming acceptable to God.

> Do you know what it means to lie down in green pastures?

If you are one of the Lord's sheep, do you know what it means to lie down in the green pastures that He has provided? It is the place where your soul is fed and you are content because your Shepherd is with you. Remember that although the illustration used in Psalm 23 is a physical one, the analogy is to the spiritual realm. Too many of God's sheep are starved in their spirit and soul because they are engrossed with their earthly circumstances and discontent with their lot in life. They fail to see with their spiritual eyes the many blessings that Christ has provided for us "in heavenly places" (Eph. 1:3) which are ours to claim by faith even when our physical circumstances are plagued with difficulty.

2. The Shepherd Gives Peace (v. 2)

Not only does the shepherd give rest in green pastures, He gently leads his sheep to quiet pools where they can drink. Sheep will not drink from fast-running water or when the flock is on the move. Many believer-sheep seem to live in a frenzy of activity. They follow their Shepherd at a distance while trying to get all they can out of this world. They have not found rest for their souls by quiet pools because they distance themselves from the Shepherd. Their ears are plugged with the world's "noise," with the result that they cannot hear His voice. They become thirsty, but they try to quench their thirst in all the wrong places (Jer. 2:13). They sip at the cup of the world's frenetic culture and don't follow the One who wants to lead them to the quiet pools of living water. The Lord Jesus beckons, "If any man is thirsty, let Him come to Me and drink" (John 7:37). The key to finding peace by the still waters is to let Him lead you there.

> The key to finding peace is to let Him lead you there.

3. The Shepherd Restores (v. 3)

Occasionally, sheep that are heavy with fleece will lie down and not be able to get up. Their center of gravity causes them to roll over, and they cannot recover without the help of the shepherd. They need to be righted again or they will die, so the shepherd restores them to their former condition. Things like disappointment, guilt, and sorrow cause us to lose heart and we find ourselves "the wrong way up." What we need is the personal ministry of the divine Shepherd to restore us, to get us back on our feet again. It is He who restores our souls and puts us back on our feet spiritually.

4. The Shepherd Directs (v. 3)

When God restores our souls, He also provides direction in the right way, the paths of righteousness. Shepherds in the Middle East do not drive their sheep; they lead them. The term *righteousness* as used here does not refer either to imputed righteousness (Rom. 5:18-19) or to the moral behavior we call righteousness (Rom. 6:13). Rather, it refers to what is right in contrast to what is wrong. Right paths are the paths along which the shepherd guides his sheep from pasture to pasture. The word "leads" in verse 3 is different from the word translated "leads" in verse 2. There, his leading beside still waters is gentle. In verse 3 it is a stronger word that implies coercion. When we wander from the path or get behind, our Shepherd will use the rod of His Word to bring us back to the right path.

Our Shepherd leads His sheep in right paths "for His name's sake." He calls them to stay near to Him because sheep's behavior reflects on the honor of the shepherd's name. If a pack of dogs kills a straggling sheep, or if a wandering sheep falls into a ravine, the shepherd's good reputation is damaged. Unfortunately, many believer-sheep pay little attention to the voice of the Shepherd calling them to stay near Him. Believers who walk in "unrighteous" paths do much to dishonor the name of their Shepherd. The solution is to listen to His voice (found by reading His Word) and to stay near Him.

5. The Shepherd Gives Courage (v. 4)

Although this verse is often used to comfort those near to death, its primary focus is to give believers courage through the dark valleys of life. Sheep in the Holy Land are transferred from place to place seasonally. The journey often takes them through dark ravines and valleys that have steep sides and deep shadows, even in the daytime. Wild animals lurk in those shadows, and occasionally floods threaten. The shadows can therefore become shadows of death. The journey through the valleys is as much a part of the Shepherd's guidance along "right paths" as the green pastures are. In fact, the way through the valley is the way *to* the green pastures.

> God's personal presence is the reason for David's confidence.

The problem in the valley is fear, the fear of unseen dangers. And the answer to that problem is to take courage. We can take courage, not because we might be lucky and slip through without being attacked or drowned, but because the Shepherd is with us. The sheep sings out, "You are with me." Notice the grammatical change: the pronouns referring to the Lord change from the third person "He" to the second person "You." The Shepherd is so near in the valley that the sheep can talk to Him directly. We are never so conscious of God's presence as we are when we are in the valley. Dangers lurk in the shadows, but He is with us. When God sent the Israelites from Mount Sinai to walk through the desert He promised them, "My Presence will go with you" (Ex. 33:14). God's personal presence is the reason for David's confidence, and it should be ours as well.

6. The Shepherd Comforts (v. 4)

The sixth provision of the shepherd relates to the two items he carries in his hand. The shepherd's rod, or club, is a weapon to beat off thieves and wild animals that may threaten the flock. David the shepherd boy probably used a rod the times he faced a lion and a bear (1 Sam. 17:34-35). The rod is also used to beat down the brush and thorn bushes to make a way for the sheep to pass through without getting their wool caught. The shepherd also carries a staff, or crook. This is used to rescue stray sheep that get caught in the rocks or in thorn bushes. Sheep, like people, sometimes do foolish things and get themselves into all kinds of trouble that might have been avoided if they had followed the shepherd. When the sheep get in trouble, the shepherd is there to rescue them. His rod and staff bring comfort to the sheep, for they know that the shepherd is well-equipped to take care of them not only in dangers and difficulties, but when they wander away willfully.

7. The Shepherd Protects (v. 5)

Some commentators think that the imagery of the life of sheep changes at this point to that of a banquet table, particularly in view of the last line of the psalm. However, even this verse can be understood in the context of a shepherd and his sheep. The image of the prepared table illustrates how the shepherd goes before his sheep to prepare the pasture for them. Before he lets them graze there, he examines it for potential or hidden dangers: he checks for poisonous weeds that would make them sick, and he inspects the pasture for fresh droppings of wild animals that might indicate their presence nearby. In this way, he "prepares a table" before the sheep so they can safely graze there.

What a picture of our caring Shepherd, the Lord Jesus Christ! As the Good Shepherd, he sought us out and found us as sheep that had gone astray. He laid down His life for us and brought us into His fold (John 10:11). He rose from the dead to become our great Shepherd. Peter calls Him the "the

Shepherd and Overseer [Guardian] of your souls" (1 Peter 2:25). What a comfort to know that our Shepherd has prepared every detail of how and where and when we can feed on the proper food that will build us up. If He triumphed over Satan, the ruler of this world, to give us life, will He not make provision for us while we remain in Satan's hostile territory? Will He not provide everything for our spiritual needs? Will He not keep us safe as the guardian of our souls (Rom. 5:10)?

8. The Shepherd Heals (v. 5)

The eighth thing that the shepherd provided for his sheep was healing. When sheep would poke around for food in the meadows, they would occasionally get scratches and cuts. The shepherd would soften the dry skin with oil to promote healing. But sheep are in still greater need of something to relieve them from the flies that torment them in the fall, particularly the nose fly. Sometimes olive oil would be mixed with sulphur and spices to make a kind of insect repellent. The careful shepherd would always have some with him and would regularly inspect the sheep to see if they needed attention. The shepherd's oil reminds us of the work of the Holy Spirit in our lives. "My cup runs over." The cup running over seems to be the cup of joy and testimony as a result of all that the Shepherd has provided for the sheep. If the anointing of the head of the sheep with oil speaks of the gracious work of the Spirit of God in our minds, then perhaps the cup that runs over speaks of the abounding joy that results (Isa. 12:2-3; Rom. 15:13).

David has listed for us eight wonderful provisions from the Shepherd for His sheep: rest, peace, restoration, direction, courage, comfort, protection, and healing. Recognizing all these provisions, the sheep would never want, or lack, any good thing, so he can exult, "My cup runs over" (cf. Ps. 45:1).

Confidence for the Future (v. 6)

The song of the sheep in the care of the shepherd comes to a close in verse 6. David has received all that his Shepherd has provided for him in the past and the present. Now he sings of the future. Not only is he convinced that the Lord will continue to provide for his needs, but he is so content that he also has no desire to ever wander from Him. David is confident that the two "guardians" of God's goodness and mercy will follow, or more literally, *pursue* him for the remainder of his life. And David's biography confirms that goodness and mercy *did* pursue him, in the wilderness of Judea, on the battlefield, and in the palace.

Although the metaphor of "the house of the Lord" refers to God's presence and provision in this life, undoubtedly David's confidence in God to care for his soul extended beyond the grave as well. And we as New Testament believers know that God has provided the most important kind of "rest" for us—the peace that comes with the forgiveness of our sins and the assurance that we will be accepted into God's own dwelling when we die (Rom. 5:1-2). At that time, the journey through this danger-filled world will end. The temporal experience of following the Shepherd through green pastures, still waters, right paths, and dark valleys, will be over. The Shepherd will lead us right into His own house to dwell forever with Him.

> The Shepherd
> will lead us into
> His own house
> to dwell forever
> with Him.

3

PSALM 27
THE LORD IS MY GUIDING LIGHT

In Psalm 27, David testifies to his great confidence in God amid life-threatening circumstances. We do not know for certain the exact context in which he wrote it, as much of his life (even as the king of Israel) was spent being pursued by enemies and being rejected in general. Traditionally it is thought that David wrote this psalm during the first seven years of his reign (in Hebron) before he was recognized by all Israel as their king. Altogether, David reigned for forty years. Although we cannot identify with most of David's physical experiences, we can identify with his emotions and the spiritual exercises of his heart. Both David and the other psalmists put into words human responses to a variety of life's experiences, like hope, fear, doubt, distress, confidence, joy, frustration, anger, and desire for justice.

The Structure of Psalm 27

Psalm 27 comprises two distinct sections. The first is a song about David's confidence in God (vv. 1-6). The second is his prayer to God for help (vv. 7-14). The transition from the first section to the second is abrupt—so much so, many Bible scholars think the two sections are two independent psalms written by different authors. However, it is best to see Psalm 27 is as one psalm, for at least three reasons: (1) the wording in both sections is remarkably similar; (2) the sudden transition at the end of verse 6 is characteristic of many other psalms; and (3) the "mood" of the psalm, swinging from faith, to fear, and back to faith again, is typical of many psalms, mirroring the cyclical experience of many believers.

David's Song of Confidence in God's Presence (vv. 1-6)

The Light of God's Presence (v. 1)

David begins by describing in two ways his personal confidence of God's presence with him: as his "light" and as "the strength of his life." The Hebrew word translated "light" refers to the realm of light rather than light as a source. The person who dwells in light is confident because he can easily see possible dangers. He can see the way ahead and is therefore unlikely to wander off the path into danger or stumble over obstacles. Righteous people love to live in "the light." Our Savior is the "Light of the world" (John 9:5). Christ provides the realm of light in which believers dwell. When we are saved we come to Christ, the Light. Then we can live and walk in the light. We have the "light of life" (John 8:12) in which to walk (by staying close to Him) and we enjoy the "light of [His] countenance [presence]" (Ps. 44:3) as well.

Living in the light provided by the Lord results in ultimate deliverance from life's problems. David, in referring to God as his "salvation," would have been thinking of God's delivering him from the many life-threatening situations he had experienced, not salvation from eternal punishment. David recognized God as the one who was preserving his physical life. In applying this verse to us spiritually, we too can rejoice in God as our light and our salvation in this life. Light signifies God's illuminating presence, and salvation signifies His mighty power to deliver us out of life's trials, often by providing us with "the way of escape" (righteous and godly choices of action and/or attitude) so that we may be able to endure them (1 Cor. 10:13). Although God *is* our Deliverer from earthly trials, the choice to make biblically wise decisions in those trials rests with us. The apostle Paul urged Christians to "walk as children of light" and to "have no fellowship with the unfruitful works of darkness" (Eph. 5:8, 11).

The Strength of God's Presence (vv. 1b-3)

David also asserts that God was "the strength of [his] life." The word *strength* contains the imagery of a fortress as a place of refuge. If David was living in Hebron at this time, he had no physical fortress. But his confidence was in the protecting presence of God, so he boasts, "Of whom shall I be afraid?" David reminds himself of God's protection in the past from wicked people who attacked him. He pictures them as wild animals who wanted to devour him but who stumbled and fell just as they were about to spring. David's confidence in God is such that even if an army attacked him, he would not be afraid. And even if a full-fledged war were to develop, his confidence in God would not be shaken (v. 3). We too can exercise courage and find strength in God to face the trials of life because the Almighty God is our protector.

> ───── ✍ ─────
> **We can exercise courage and find strength in God to face the trials of life.**
> ───── ✍ ─────

Desire for God's Presence (v. 4)

From his calm confidence in God's presence, even though surrounded by enemies, David expresses his one deep desire to draw near to God and worship Him. Whatever his circumstances were at the time he wrote this psalm, it appears that he had no access to the "house of the LORD," meaning the tent tabernacle in Shiloh. (It was David's son, Solomon, who built the temple in Jerusalem.) It was there at the tabernacle that worshippers could draw near to God with their sacrifices and offerings. The desire of David's heart was to worship his God. Doing so helped him be God-centered and not occupied with himself.

The word "inquire" carries the imagery of eagerly watching through the night for the light of the morning. Thus, to dwell in God's presence is to eagerly seek Him as we might look for the sunrise. For us as New Testament believers it is to concentrate on the glories of our crucified and risen Savior, the Lord Jesus Christ. It is to come with our offerings of praise and be conscious of the Lord's presence among His people. Then we may catch a glimpse of the glory of God in the face of Jesus Christ. And when we "see" Him, we will worship and adore Him.

Security in God's Presence (v. 5)

David links his personal safety with the tabernacle because it was there that God had established His presence among His people; God's presence was symbolized by the tabernacle, and the benefit of being in God's presence is what was on David's mind. David would not have been allowed into the inner rooms of the tabernacle as he was not a priest, so he is not speaking here of being literally hidden in the tabernacle. In the early days of King Solomon's reign, Joab, one of his generals, defected from him to Adonijah, another of David's sons, who aspired to be king. When Solomon heard of this, Joab fled to the tabernacle and took hold of the horns of the altar hoping for safety (1 Kings 2:28). However, there was no safety for him there because he was guilty.

David was confident that God would look after *him,* however, because he was counted among the righteous. He uses another word picture of safekeeping in verse 5 by saying that he felt as safe as if God had lifted him high on a rock, well away from anyone trying to harm him.

Response to God's Presence (v. 6)

David's confidence gives him a sense of victory over his enemies. He exults, "And now my head shall be lifted up above my enemies all around me." Thus David had the assurance both of Yahweh's presence near him and pleasure *in* him. With these

—— ✐ ——

We should express heartfelt worship to the Lord.

—— ✐ ——

assurances in mind, he closes this section with a promise to respond in two ways: first, to offer sacrifices at the Lord's tabernacle, and second, to sing praises to Him (v. 6). David does not view his accession to the throne as an opportunity for personal glory. Rather, if God gives him the victory, he sees it as reason to worship. For him, the consuming passion of his soul was to worship Yahweh. David sets us a good example here. As New Testament believers, we should take advantage of the many hymns that have been written through the ages to express our own heartfelt worship to the Lord.

David's Prayer for God's Presence (vv. 7-12)

It is at this point in the psalm that David's frame of mind seems to change dramatically. He goes from being confident in God and delighting in His presence to being in doubt about whether God is near and whether He is even listening. He prays, "Hear, O LORD, when I cry with my voice! Have mercy also upon me, and answer me." He has gone from confidence to anxiety, from faith to fear, from singing to soul-searching. These two extremes are nearer to each other than we sometimes think. When we allow circumstances to affect our fellowship with God, it is only a short step from faith to fear.

David may well have become anxious about the long war between his supporters and those of the house of Saul (2 Sam. 3:1). Whatever the actual circumstance, his mood changed from faith to fear. Peter experienced a similar change of mood when, at the invitation of the Lord Jesus, he walked on the stormy waters of Lake Galilee. When he took his eyes off Jesus and noticed the waves, his faith turned to fear and he immediately began to sink (Matt. 14:30). When David took *his* eyes off God, he began to fear.

Fear of Losing God's Presence (v. 8)

David knew that God was asking him to seek His face (v. 8, 105:4), that is, the consciousness of God's presence. We read in other psalms the same phrase, "Do not hide Your face from me" (v. 9, cf. 69:17, 102:2, 143:7). In contrast to that, the priestly blessing on Israel is "The LORD, make His face shine upon you" and "lift up His countenance upon you" (Num. 6:25-26). This blessing is echoed three times in Psalm 80: "Cause Your face to shine" (vv. 3, 7, 19). So we should respond in faith with David by saying, "Your face, LORD, I will seek."

> ———— ❧ ————
> **"Your face, LORD,
> I will seek."**
> **–Psalm 27:8**
> ———— ❧ ————

David does not yet sense God's face, or presence, so He prays, "Do not hide Your face from me; Do not turn Your servant away in anger. . . . Do not leave me nor forsake me" (v. 9). He feels forsaken; he senses that God is far away. Sometimes God seems to hide His face from us, and we realize how destitute we are without it. When this is our experience, He leads us to a greater degree of trust than we have attempted before. The Gentile woman of Mark 7:28 is an apt illustration here. She begged Christ to cast the demon out of her daughter. But He did not at first give her the blessing she sought. He told her that it was not good to throw the children's bread to the dogs (Jews being equated to "children," and Gentiles to "dogs"). She humbly replied that even the little dogs under the table ate the children's crumbs. And because of she humbled herself and expressed faith in His mercy, Christ granted her request.

From Faith, to Fear, to Faith (vv. 9-10)

Notice that David's pleadings for God's presence are interspersed with statements of his trust (vv. 9-10). This is another example of vacillating between fear and faith.

> "Do not hide Your face from me; Do not turn Your servant away in anger;
>
> *You have been my help;*
>
> Do not leave me nor forsake me,
>
> *O God of my salvation.*
>
> When my father and my mother forsake me,
>
> *Then the LORD will take care of me.*"

"Take care of me" (v. 10) is the language of a parent who lifts up his or her child to provide for its needs. In the same way, our heavenly Father lifts us up when earthly help seems to fail us. Think of Ishmael's mother, who put her son under a bush because he was dying of thirst (Gen. 21:8-21). The Lord took care of him. Or think of Moses' parents, who committed their baby son to the ark in the River Nile (Ex. 2:1-10). The Lord took care of him as well. So we can say with assurance along with David, "The Lord will take care of me."

A Prayer for God's Help (vv. 11-12)

David prays for two things: to know how to please God and for protection from his enemies. From praying *negatively* ("Do not hide ... do not turn away ... do not leave me"), David now prays *positively,* asking to be taught God's way, to be led in God's path, and to be preserved by God's protection.

"Teach me Your way"

David wants to be shown the way that pleases God. Moses had been in a similar situation as David when he was up on the mountain with God for forty days at Mount Sinai. It was there that God spoke with him "face to face" (Ex. 33:11). God told Moses to lead the Israelites through the wilderness to the Promised Land. Then Moses responded like David, "Show me now Your way." So God promised, "My Presence will go with you." The themes of God's presence, God's way, and God's grace are the same in both cases. When we too desire God's presence, we need to seek His "way" as opposed to our own.

"Lead me in a smooth path"

David asks to be lead on a plain or smooth pathway—a level open road. The concept is that of a road which runs through enemy territory. Unwary travelers are liable

> We need to seek God's "way" as opposed to our own.

to be attacked if they travel such a road. A civil war in Sri Lanka prompted the government to clear the road through tropical jungle for half a mile on each side so that the enemy forces could not easily ambush passing vehicles. The civilians who traveled that road were thankful for the clear and open road. They felt more confident of arriving safely at their destination as a result of it. David prayed for a plain path so that his enemies could not ambush him. Note that he did not pray for an *easy* path.

"Deliver me"

If David's enemies could not destroy him with weapons, they would try to do it with words. Tongues are often more to be feared than swords. Think of the havoc that tongues have caused among communities of believers through the years! In Psalm 35:11 David calls them "fierce witnesses."

In verse 2 the enemies are likened to wild beasts. Here in verse 12 they are false witnesses who slander him and threaten him. David faced false witnesses against him while he lived in Hebron. They wanted to make Saul's son Ishbosheth the king instead of David. But he waited for God's time and would not answer back to his enemies with either sharp swords or sharp words. And God answered his prayer for deliverance without David having to scheme to accomplish it himself. He removed Abner, Saul's general, and Ishbosheth, Saul's son, from blocking David's way to becoming king over all Israel. David prayed "deliver me," and God did it.

David's Declaration of His Faith in God's Goodness (vv. 13-14)

David says, "I would have lost heart, unless I had believed that I would see the goodness of the LORD in the land of the living." In Psalm 23, viewing God as his shepherd, David believed that "goodness and mercy [would] follow [him] all the days of [his] life" (Ps. 23:6). The "land of the living" has to do with life while we are still on earth. We can be confident, like David, that even though we will go through trials in this life, the blessings of God outweigh the bad things we endure. God is always good *and* good to us.

David ends his psalm with an exhortation to both his own soul and the believing community to learn the lesson of waiting on the Lord. If God does not immediately direct your steps and does not immediately deliver you from your difficulties—what then? Have you considered waiting? Yes, God often calls us to wait for Him to act. It takes faith and patience to wait quietly for Him to act on our behalf. When you do this, God will encourage (strengthen) your heart, and in the meantime you can delight in His presence with you.

4

PSALM 32
THE LORD IS MY FORGIVING JUDGE

Psalm 32 deals with the important topic of restoring our fellowship with God when sin has damaged it. It is known as one of the seven "penitential" psalms. These are psalms that deal with the sense of guilt we have when we come to terms with our sin and its offence against our holy God; when we sorrow for the sin, confess it, and are willing to change our ways.

Historical Background

The author of Psalm 32 is David, as the title indicates. This leads many commentators to believe that its theme of sins forgiven flows out of his own personal experience of committing adultery and murder and his subsequent repentance. We read in 2 Samuel 11 the account of how King David seduced Bathsheba, the wife of Uriah, a loyal soldier. When David learned that she was pregnant with his child, he arranged for Uriah to be assigned to the front of the battle, where he soon perished. David then married Bathsheba. For nearly a year he pretended that everything was well, but during that time his soul was, in fact, haunted by guilt.

Eventually God sent the prophet Nathan to confront him with his sin and to announce the discipline God had ordered. David responded by fully confessing his sin and genuinely repenting from it (2 Sam. 12:1-20). God immediately forgave him, allowing spiritual fellowship between them to be restored. David wrote his confession and prayer in Psalm 51, in which he promised that he would teach other transgressors the ways of God (Ps. 51:13). He kept his promise when he later wrote this psalm, which contains that teaching.

Psalm 32's Relevance to Believers Today

Christians are those who have believed that the Lord Jesus Christ died for the guilt of their sin. Until we trust Christ as Savior we are reckoned guilty before a holy God whether we *feel* guilty or not. As we grow spiritually, the Holy Spirit teaches us to have an increasing sensitivity to the sins we commit in order to purify us. Whether or not we, as believers,

> ─────── ❦ ───────
> **The Holy Spirit teaches us to have an increasing sensitivity to the sins we commit.**
> ─────── ❦ ───────

ever commit the magnitude of sin that David did, we can identify with the joy and blessing David experienced of sins forgiven.

The title calls Psalm 32 a *Maskil*, meaning, "for contemplation or teaching." We learn several important truths about sin and the believer in this psalm. What happens when we sin? What happens if we try to ignore the fact that we have sinned? What happens when we confess our sin to God? These are wonderful truths that have blessed God's people for thirty centuries. Each of us should carefully consider the implications for our own life in our relationship with our holy God.

The Blessing of Forgiveness (vv. 1-2a)

David pronounces in the first verse that the forgiven person is a "blessed" one. The blessed person is not he who is simply happy, but one with a deep, inner sense of satisfaction that God has dealt well with him. Here in Psalm 32 the blessed person is the one, like David, who embraces the blessing of full forgiveness for sins committed.

Three Descriptions of Sin

The first two verses contain some great biblical truths about sin and God's remedies for it. We will look at them in detail, though we should not forget that this is Hebrew poetry and not a theological passage. Notice, first, the three words used that describe sin: *transgression, sin,* and *iniquity.* Understanding the difference in these terms helps us grasp how many ways we can express disobedience to a holy God. (1) To transgress is to deliberately cross the line between right and wrong doing. To cross that line is to basically rebel against the revealed will of God and His authority. (2) To sin means to deviate from a path, the path that is well pleasing to God. It has also been defined as "missing the mark," as in a target. (3) The term "iniquity" has to do with the inward perversion of our nature that manifests itself in wrongdoing.

Allusions to the Day of Atonement

These three terms for sin all appear in the instructions for observing the annual Day of Atonement that God prescribed for Israel. The high priest would, along with a number of other sacrifices, make atonement on that day for the sins of the people by sacrificing a goat on the brazen altar. He would then sprinkle some of the blood on and before the mercy seat on the Ark of the Covenant in the Holy of Holies (the inner room in the tabernacle). The high priest would then lay his hands on a second (live) goat and confess over it all the *iniquities* of the children of Israel, all their *transgressions,* and all their *sins* (Lev. 16:20-22). That goat would then be driven away into the wilderness. We read in that passage that "the goat shall bear on itself all their iniquities."

New Testament Fulfillment

In John 1:29, John the Baptist said of Jesus, "Behold! The Lamb of God who *takes away* the sin of the world!" (emphasis added). Christ was the scapegoat. In John's first letter he states that "the blood of Jesus Christ cleanses us from all sin" (1 John 1:7). Christ was the atoning sacrifice for sin who completely *cleanses* us from sin—He doesn't just *cover* it. The apostle Peter said that it was Jesus Christ "who Himself bore our sins in His own body on the tree" (1 Peter 2:24), and Paul said in 2 Corinthians 5:21 that God "made Him [Christ] who knew no sin to be sin for us, that we might become the righteousness of God in Him." Sins are no longer charged to the believer because Jesus, the sinless substitute, paid the price for them.

> Christ was the atoning sacrifice for sin who *completely* cleanses us from sin.

Sin Forgiven, Covered, and Not Imputed

Notice how each of the descriptions of sin is linked in Psalm 32 to one of God's remedies for it. First, transgressions are "forgiven," which means "sent away." Our transgressions are carried away, as seen in the scapegoat of Leviticus 16. Second, the remedy for "sin" is to provide a covering (atonement) for it so that God no longer "sees" our sin. This was symbolized by the sprinkling (covering) of sacrificial blood before the mercy seat.

Finally, the remedy for iniquity is that it is not imputed or counted against the guilty ones, as their sinful nature makes them completely unable to make themselves righteous. In Old Testament times as well as New, the "righteous" person was justified by faith in God. Paul gave two examples of justification by faith in Old Testament times in his epistle to the Romans: first, of Abraham, whose belief in the Lord was reckoned to him as righteousness, and second, of David, to whom God imputed (credited) righteousness without works so that his faith was accounted for righteousness (Rom. 4:5-7). The great plan of salvation allows God to be, as Romans 3:26 says, both just and the justifier of the one who has faith in Jesus.

God no longer holds the believer accountable for his sin. He is forgiven, cleansed, and justified in God's sight!

The Prerequisite for Forgiveness (v. 2b)

The final phrase of verse 2, "And in whose spirit there is no deceit," refers to the condition (attitude) of the sinning believer. He does not hide his sin; instead, he honestly confesses it to God. It is the nature of sin to deceive, as Satan is a deceiver (John 8:44). When we commit sin, we often rationalize in our minds its seriousness, harm, or effect. The penitent Christian will deal honestly with himself and with God and not cover up his sin. He will acknowledge it for what it is and agree with God in condemning it.

David's Experience of Forgiveness (vv. 3-5)

In the psalm, David now testifies as to how God brought him to the place of spiritual blessedness. He begins, "When I kept silent," referring to his failure to confess his sin. He may have kept quiet because of pride or perhaps out of fear of shame and damage to his reputation. He was silent as to confession, but not in his pain. Although he did not lose his status of being counted righteous in God's sight, he certainly lost the joy of that position. Guilt took its toll on his body and his emotions. He acknowledges that God's disciplinary hand was heavy upon him in remorse for the death of his friend and in shame for his sexual sin. "Selah!" is an expression used often in the psalms for a time to reflect during a musical interlude. Sometimes it marks a new direction in the flow of thought. Sometimes, as here, it means, "Just think about that!"

It was at that point that David's proud spirit was broken. His cover-up had failed. When faced with Nathan's accusation, "You are the man!" (2 Sam. 12:7), he confessed (agreed about) it. He exulted in how God had handled his transgression, his sin, his iniquity. God forgave it, covered it, and did not make him pay for it. Now he tells how he confessed to God the same three synonyms for sin. He acknowledged his sin, he confessed his transgression, and he did not hide his iniquity. He did not simply tell of the sins, but specifically confessed "*my* sin," "*my* iniquity" and "*my* transgressions."

David confessed clearly to God: "Against You, You only, have I sinned" (Ps. 51:4). And in faith David could now triumphantly state, "You forgave the iniquity of my sin." Right here he interjected the term "Selah." Just think of that. And so it is with the Christian. If we confess our sin, He is faithful and just to forgive us our sin and to cleanse us from all unrighteousness. He does this on the basis of Christ's all-sufficient work on the cross. Notice at the end of verse 5, where David says that God lifted the "iniquity," literally, the "guilt." Being forgiven means that the sin is no longer an issue with God; it therefore needs not plague our body, mind, or spirit. David teaches from his own experience that the way out of anguish is unreserved confession of the sin.

David Exhorts the Godly (vv. 6-7)

David's experience of forgiveness motivates him to exhort others to prove the Lord in the same way that he had. Thus, based on his experience he says, "For this cause." He instructs the godly to seek the blessing of forgiveness as well. Author Jerry Bridges has

———— ✍ ————

Devotion to God is the mainspring of godly character.

———— ✍ ————

written that "devotion to God is the mainspring of godly character." The believer who is devoted to God is one who is increasingly sensitive to sin in his life; he is one who "keeps short accounts" with God over them. In other words, he confesses them as soon as the indwelling Spirit convicts him.

The godly have no need to worry about the coming judgment that is illustrated in verse 6 by "a flood of great waters." The godly have a "hiding place" of protection, and that hiding place is God Himself. This phrase is applied to God in several other psalms (27:5, 31:20, 91:1). Many psalms speak of God as a means of protection from harm (refuge, rock, fortress, etc), but the term "hiding place" (also translated "secret place") goes a step further: when God is our hiding-place, we are not only safe from harm, *we cannot even be found.* In the context of the coming judgment for sin, the picture conveys just how secure we are as a forgiven people. In New Testament terms, we are "in Christ," which is to be as accepted and acceptable to God as Christ, the spotless Son of God is!

Satan will often seek to rob us of the joy of sins forgiven by bringing them back to mind. It is by faith that we must then remind ourselves that God's forgiveness is bound up in His promises in His Word and His Son's work on the cross. We enjoy God's permanent protection from both future eternal judgment and present feelings of guilt. This is pictured

> The blessing of having our sins forgiven is security for eternity and peace in our heart for today.

here as being surrounded with "songs [or shouts] of deliverance." God preserves us from "trouble," better translated "distress." The blessing of having our sins forgiven is security for eternity and peace in our heart for today (Rom. 5:1-2).

God Instructs the Forgiven Saint (vv. 8-9)

Commentators are not all agreed that God is the speaker in verse 8. Some think that David is the speaker and that he is teaching those who have found a hiding place in the Lord. It is better to understand that God is speaking, especially considering the phrase, "I will guide you with My eye." God is responding to David's confidence in Him. Looking at it this way, God gives him three great promises for the future. God's forgiveness and protection were not to be the climax of his life for God; rather, they were to mark a new beginning for the future. As a forgiven sinner he would then enjoy God's instruction, teaching, and counsel.

The effectiveness of David's service for God was to come from his ongoing submission to God. He would learn what the will of God was from the instruction, teaching, and counsel that God would give him. In this way he would gain knowledge and wisdom to apply God's truth to the circumstances of his life. First, God would instruct him and teach him in the way of righteousness. The forgiven sinner does not automatically act righteously in every situation, but must be taught, line upon line. God does this through His Word as it is read, taught, meditated on, and explained. Having been taught and instructed, he should gladly follow in God's ways.

The next phrase tells us that God promises to guide His people with His eye. This means that God will keep watch over us individually. Some schoolteachers see the special giftedness of particular students and keep an eye on them so as to help their progress and to counsel them effectively. God keeps watch over us for our best good and for His own glory. He is the God whose eye is on the sparrow, and He watches over those who are of more value that many sparrows (Matt. 10:31). And as God watches over us, we should be carefully listening to His still, small voice.

We are not to be like horses and mules, which have to be forcibly guided by means of bit and bridle because they do not understand their owner's intentions. God is perfectly capable of forcing us to do His will, either to stop some course of action or to start another. Too often we are like a restless horse stamping its feet in frustration. How much better to hear God's voice and respond with willing obedience than have to be forced into obedience through one of God's harsher disciplines. Do we want to be treated like people or like horses and mules? The last phrase in verse 9 is unclear, so some have suggested it be translated "lest he kick against you." That seems to make sense but is not indicated in text.

God Blesses the Righteous (vv. 10-11)

In the final two verses of this psalm there is a strong contrast between the sorrows of the wicked and the joy of the righteous. The "wicked" may temporarily seem to prosper, but they will also have many sorrows, sorrows that do not necessarily lead him to repentance and faith. Those sorrows will not be limited to this life, but will carry on into eternity. But he who trusts in Yahweh in this life will be surrounded by God's mercy in this life *and* in the next. Living in the realm of God's unfailing love is among the great promises of Scripture.

In the seventh verse the faithful are said to be surrounded by songs of deliverance. But in the last verse of the psalm there is another circle. It is a ring of God's mercies that surround the faithful so that the evil one cannot get through to hurt them. The wicked are the unbelieving who do not heed the counsel of God, and the "righteous" are those who believe in God and are forgiven. The righteous and the wicked are seen in this light all through the Psalms.

In the final verse there is another threesome of words that describe a crescendo of joy for the righteous—the forgiven believers who are surrounded by God's loving-kindness. They are to be "glad in the Lord," referring to the inward sense of joy concerning something good. They are to "rejoice," an outward expression that sometimes includes the idea of joyful actions. And they are to "shout for joy" as in singing a victory song.

5

PSALM 34
THE LORD IS MY STRONG
DELIVERER

This is the first of two psalms that flow from David's experience in a Philistine prison after having fled as a fugitive from Israel. Psalm 56 is his *prayer* for deliverance, and Psalm 34 is his *praise* for deliverance.

Historical Background

The event that occasioned this psalm is evident from its title: "The psalm of David when he pretended madness before Abimelech, when he drove him away, and he departed." Israel won a great battle when David killed the giant Goliath. As a result, King Saul invited him to live in his palace. This is where Prince Jonathan befriended him. During the celebration of victory over the Philistines, the women praised David more than King Saul. They sang, "Saul has slain his thousands, and David his ten thousands" (1 Sam. 18:7), causing Saul to become jealous of David. He tried to try to kill him but, with Jonathan's help, David fled to the Philistine city of Gath out of fear for his life, seeking refuge from Achish, the Philistine king (Abimelech is the generic title of Philistine kings). Read 1 Samuel 21:10-16.

When Achish discovered who David was, David grew afraid of what the king might do to him. But instead of trusting God, he sought to save himself. He did this by deceiving Achish into thinking he was insane. He scribbled on the doors and let his saliva run down his beard. King Achish fell for David's trick and became disgusted with him. According to the heading of the psalm, he wanted nothing to do with David, and he drove him away. David had no choice but to go back to Israel and live as a fugitive from King Saul. He hid in a cave near the town of Adullam. News of his whereabouts reached some friends, who secretly came to join him. They believed that David would be Israel's next king. First his family came, then sympathizers, debtors, and those who were discontented with Saul's rule (1 Sam. 22:1-2). But the best thing that happened was that David was restored to the Lord, as we see expressed in Psalm 34.

Psalm 34 is one of nine acrostic psalms. These are psalms in which the first word begins with the letters of the Hebrew alphabet in order. There are twenty-two verses in this psalm, and each begins with a succeeding letter of the Hebrew alphabet. Psalm 119 is the best known of the acrostic psalms; each section of eight verses begins with successive letters of the alphabet. The purpose of writing acrostics was to help people to memorize them.

———— ✍ ————

The best antidote to complaining and depression is to praise God

———— ✍ ————

David Praises the Lord (vv. 1-2)

David begins with a promise (almost a vow) that he will bless the Lord at all times. To bless God (as opposed to Him blessing us) is to joyfully praise Him in response to His gracious dealings with us. The Lord had mercifully delivered David twice: first from King Saul, and then from King Achish.

David said he would bless God continually. New Testament believers are exhorted in Hebrews 13:15 to "continually offer the sacrifice of praise to God, that is, the fruit of our lips, giving thanks to His name." The word "boast" in verse 2 is the Hebrew word *halal* from which we get the word "hallelujah." It is used 165 times in the Old Testament, most often translated "praise." David's soul would continue to boast about the Lord until even the humble (meaning those who had joined him in fleeing from Saul) would hear of it and be glad with him (v. 2).

David Invites Others to Praise the Lord (v. 3)

The best antidote to complaining and depression is to praise God. David invites his companions to join him in magnifying the Lord and exalting His name (v. 3). To magnify the Lord is to make Him great. To exalt His name is to raise it up above everything else in the eyes of all created beings, including the unseen principalities and powers. Mary the mother of Jesus used this language when she heard the prophetic song of Elizabeth. She responded, "My soul magnifies the Lord, and my spirit has rejoiced in God my Savior" (Luke 1:46-47). The words in our psalm, "Let us exalt His name together," indicate the unity of purpose for a group. Together, whether as married couples, families, ministry partners, or congregations, we are to praise and magnify our God. David taught his men to praise God along with him, for they had all come from hard circumstances (1 Sam. 22:2). Praising God in company with other like-minded believers is one of the blessings of belonging to God's people and an important reason to regularly meet together in our local churches.

David Testifies about God's Deliverance (vv. 4-7)

David now turns to testifying to God's faithfulness. He gives personal testimony in verse 4 and then states a premise in verse 5, the truth of which he illustrates again from his own experience in verse 6. He had been fearful of King Achish when the king learned that he was the one who had slain Goliath, the champion of the Philistine army. God answered his prayer and delivered him from his fear even before He delivered him from King Achish. The bondage of fear is worse than the bondage of iron doors; freedom from fear is more important than freedom from difficult circumstances.

It is an often-repeated principle in the Psalms that God delivers from trouble those who call upon Him for help. The result of being delivered from trouble is a sense of blessing and of openly giving glory to God (v. 5), just as David did at the beginning of

Freedom from fear is more important than freedom from difficult circumstances.

the psalm. In verse 6 David sees himself as a "poor" (or, oppressed) man who knew from his own experience that God hears and answers pleas for help in an hour of need.

The term "the Angel of the LORD" occurs several times in the Old Testament and refers to pre-incarnate appearances of the Son of God, the second Person of the Trinity (cf. Genesis 16:7-11, 22:11, Exodus 3:2, Joshua 5:13-15, etc.). David believed that God sent the Commander of the Lord's hosts to protect those who committed themselves into His care in faith. The Angel of the Lord's protection is so thorough and complete that "He" (singular) is pictured as being able to encamp "all around" those who fear

Him. As New Testament believers, God's own Spirit dwells within us today, and we have God's assurance in Hebrews 13:5, "I will never leave you nor forsake you."

David Testifies about God's Provision (vv. 8-10)

David now appeals to others to "taste and see that the Lord is good." Some people never know how delicious a certain food may be because they refuse to try it. David urges others to find out for themselves how gracious and good God is—to experience for themselves God's delivering power and protection. To taste that the Lord is good is a step of faith. When we believe in what God promises and act on our belief, our faith-in-action will bring God's blessing on us. David had believed and found this to be true. So he encourages us with, "Blessed is the man who trusts in Him!" (v. 8).

God's "saints" should fear the Lord (v. 9). In fearing Him we will humbly walk in His laws, we will diligently do His will, and we will be careful not to offend Him. Those who do fear Him in these ways will never lack anything they need to fulfill His will. We should not miss the truth that His provision is for those who have responded to His call to fear Him: "Oh, fear the LORD, you His saints!" Old lions may no longer be able to catch their game, but young lions are fast and strong. They almost never go hungry. They symbolize self-sufficiency and human ingenuity, but cunning and strength may not be enough. Those who fear the Lord will never lack anything they need because they trust in God rather than in their own capacities.

David Instructs His Followers (vv. 11-14)

In the second section of the psalm, David gives instruction to the refugees from Israel who had attached themselves to him in the cave of Adullam. According to 1 Samuel 22:2, this group soon numbered four hundred. They loved David and admired him. They were willing to follow him anywhere and to risk their lives for him. But David realized that for this group to live in harmony and accomplish any united purpose, they had to have regulated behavior and rules. So he gathered them around him to instruct them. He uses the format of wisdom teaching, much like that of Solomon in the early chapters of the book of Proverbs. He speaks to them as a father to his children, "Come, you children, listen to me." And as children they accept his authority and submit to his teaching. This is a good model for all parents who want to see their children grow up to love and serve God.

Speak the Truth

David gives his men some strong motives for listening to him and learning the fear of the Lord (v. 12). He reminds them of some basic things that most people tend to want out of life. These have to do with the quality of life that God meant man to enjoy when He created him. Like David, these men feared God. They believed that God had chosen David to be their king. So David asks them in this verse if they really wanted the life God had planned for them and wanted to live long and live well. And if they did really want this blessed life, then this is the way to get it.

David's first lesson is to teach them that the fear of the Lord is connected to wholesome speech and actions. David has learned this, so now he can teach it. All the facets comprised in the concept of "fearing the Lord" should be central to our instruction to those coming after us, because it is the beginning of wisdom (Ps. 111:10).

> The tongue is an enormously powerful force for evil.

The great principles of living in harmony as a group and as a nation would be determined by the integrity of what these men *said* and *did*. They were to keep their tongues from any form of evil; they were to control their tongues by rejecting what was not true and speaking only truth. They must realize that the tongue is an enormously powerful force for evil; it must therefore be carefully guarded (James 4:6). The parallel statement in verse 13 intensifies the importance of truthfulness. They must keep their lips from speaking guile (deceit). David had deceived the priest Ahimelech into thinking that he was on urgent business for King Saul. He had deceived King Achish into thinking that he was insane. Now his deceitful tactics weighed on his mind, and he taught his men that when they speak, they must speak the truth.

Seek Peace

David next counsels his men to "depart from evil and do good; seek peace and pursue it." Note that it is not enough to abstain from doing something wrong; we must actively do what is "good" as well. The admonition to seek peace—to actively *pursue* peace—implies doing all in our power to be a peacemaker. It certainly includes the idea that we should not ever be the *source* of conflict or dissension.

The key to healthy relationships and a full and satisfying life is integrity in speech and actions. David was ashamed of having told those lies and pretending to be insane. Ahimelech the priest died because of his lying. King Achish became a life-long enemy of David's because of his deceit. Now David wants his men to learn from his mistakes by controlling their speech and actions. They didn't know it then, but they would be constantly under pressure in the wilderness of Judea for at least the next ten years. If they were going to live harmoniously together under these circumstances, integrity was going to be vitally important in all that they said and did.

> The key to healthy relationships and a full and satisfying life is integrity in speech and actions.

The apostle Peter quoted David's advice a thousand years later when he wrote to believers in Asia Minor. Peter knew that in light of growing hostility to the Christian faith, those believers needed to bond together and get along with one another—just like David's men at Adullam. Blessed are the peacemakers (Matt. 5:11) *and* peace-seekers!

David Testifies of God's Faithful Care (vv. 15-22)

David now summarizes his instruction to his men. He reminds them that God cares for the righteous and blesses them. But he balances this truth with the reality that the righteous may suffer in this life. The fear of the Lord is indeed the key to joy and blessing, but joy and blessing do not guarantee trouble-free lives for the righteous. The "righteous" are mentioned here four times in their relationship to God. We do well to think about them.

First, *the Lord knows and sees us* (vv. 15-16). How comforting, that no matter how difficult life may get, God is fully aware of every detail and His ears are open to our faintest whisper. We may be tempted to envy those who do evil and who seem to prosper, but we should remember that nothing they do is hidden from His sight; they will receive the just judgment due them in the end.

Second, *the Lord hears us and is near to us* (vv. 17-18). He is present with us even when we are overcome with trouble. He does not always protect us from going through trouble, but He is with us *in* our trials and delivers us out of them when His purpose has been accomplished in us. Those troubles sometimes include a broken heart, but He is still near. The most often repeated promise in the Bible is, "I am with you." The "contrite spirit" is the humility to accept what God has allowed and thereby be saved from blaming God for the present trials (v. 18).

The third truth about the Lord's relationship to the righteous is, *the Lord delivers the righteous from afflictions* (vv. 19-20). Like the *external* circumstantial troubles referred to in the previous verse, so are the internal afflictions that plague us from within our minds, bodies, and emotions. Some people are limited in their ability to function normally due to disease and depression. But in God's good time, deliverance will come—though it may not be as soon as we might choose.

Obviously verse 20 can only be applied to believers in a spiritual sense, in that though we may be afflicted in our flesh, the "framework" of our relationship to God remains unbroken. This verse had a very important prophetic purpose, however—one that David would have been unaware of when the Spirit inspired him to write it. It is quoted in John 19:36 in fulfillment of the fact that the bones of the Lord Jesus Christ were not broken by the Roman soldiers to hasten His death. The Lord dismissed His own spirit when He had fulfilled His mission of bearing God's judgment for our sins. He was therefore already dead when the soldiers went to break His legs. To fulfill the standards set for the lamb sacrificed at Passover, it was necessary that none of His bones be broken (Ex. 12:46).

The fourth truth about the relationship of God to the righteous is that *the Lord redeems the righteous and condemns the wicked (vv. 21-22).* The wicked, who hate the righteous, will ultimately face God and be judged. God always has the last word. But the righteous will escape the condemnation and be delivered from judgment because they have put their trust in God who accepted His Son's payment for sin on the cross. "There is therefore now no condemnation to those who are in Christ Jesus" (Rom. 8:1). God is their Deliverer.

6

PSALM 42 & 43
THE LORD IS MY CERTAIN HOPE

Psalms 42 and 43 articulate the intense longing for God felt by believers whose circumstances have made God seem far away. These two psalms were probably originally combined as one, even though they are separated in many early manuscripts. There are several reasons for thinking this. First, the repetition of the same refrain in them both indicates unity (see 42:5 & 11 and 43:5). Second, the repeated development of the same theme from lament to hope in both psalms shows remarkable similarity. Third, there is no superscription in the second of them, indicating that the superscription of Psalm 42 covers both. We will treat them as a whole.

Historical Background

Commentators have several suggestions as to the identity of the author. These include King Hezekiah when he was struck with a deathly illness, King Jehoiachin on his way to exile in Babylon, and King David during his flight from Absalom. David is to be preferred; as Spurgeon remarks, "It bears the marks of his style and experience in every letter," and this is the approach we will take in this lesson.

Superscription and Structure

Psalm 42 is superscripted "To the Chief Musician" or temple choir director, so it was intended to be sung in the tabernacle or temple services. The singers were "sons of Korah." When their ancestor, Korah, tried to usurp the priesthood by offering incense, he was swallowed up in the earth, but his sons were spared. The descendants of Korah's sons became temple guardians and the temple singers and musicians (Num. 16:31-35, 26:11). The headings of Psalms 42 through 49 all indicate they were written for these Korahite musicians. Four of these psalms, including this one, were "maskil" or "contemplation" psalms, meaning they were for instruction.

There are clearly three sections in the two psalms—42:1-5, 42:6-11, and 43:1-5—each with the same structure. They begin with a prayer of lament to God because He seems distant from His servant; from the writer's perspective, God seems to have forgotten him and rejected him. After each of his prayers lamenting his loneliness, he addresses his own soul with a question, "Why are you cast down, O my soul?" Finally, he exhorts his soul to "hope in God" (42:5, 11, 43:5).

God Is My Only Hope (42:1-5)

David Senses His Need of God (42:1-2)

David laments losing the sense of God's presence. He uses a thirsty deer as an illustration of his intense thirst for God. Just as a deer needs water for life, so David needed the assurance of God's presence with him. The thirsty deer panting for water is the keynote of the psalm. Christians in difficult circumstances who sense that God is far

> The human spirit cannot be satisfied until it is assured of God's personal presence!

away from them have found comfort from these words because they can identify with the psalmist. How many believers down through the centuries have come to understand that the human spirit cannot be satisfied until it is assured of God's personal presence! As if to recognize this need, the promise of God's presence with His people is the most common promise to be found in the Bible. God's promises are meant to be believed and claimed—and when they are, the result is rest for the soul.

David's Enemies Sneer at God (42:3)

The Lord Jesus said, "If anyone thirsts, let him come to Me and drink" (John 7:37). Unfortunately, we Christians are prone to try and quench our thirst from other sources. We seek satisfaction from the dry wells of pleasure, possessions, and power. Through Jeremiah the prophet, God accused His people: "They have forsaken Me, the fountain of living waters, and hewn themselves cisterns—broken cisterns that can hold no water" (Jer. 2:13). David said, "My soul thirsts for God, for the living God." Nothing but God Himself would meet his soul's craving. Although man's soul is only truly satisfied when filled by God Himself, not everyone senses this longing for Him. The truth is, it is those who have experienced it who best understand such a craving.

David describes his personal sorrow and emptiness by the phrase, "My tears have been my food day and night" (v. 3). Not only is he perplexed by his unfulfilled thirst for God, he is dismayed that his enemies are taunting him with the question, "Where is your God?"

> God always has an ultimate purpose in everything that He allows.

The same taunt is still used by unbelievers in time of disaster or tragedy. But the answer is that God is just where He has always been—on the throne of the universe and in full control. He always has an ultimate purpose in everything that He allows.

David Recalls Past Joys (42:4)

David had sunk into depression because he was focusing on himself, pouring out his soul *within him* rather than pouring out his heart to God. Then he remembered better days—particularly the pilgrimages to Jerusalem for the three great festivals of Passover, Pentecost, and Booths (Tabernacles). He recalled his part in the processions—joyful times of singing with thanksgiving as he joined with the faithful in praise to God.

David Exhorts His Own Soul to Hope in God (42:5)

David now speaks to his own heart. His faith questions his fears. "Why are you cast down, O my soul?" Why are you so depressed? It is a good thing to examine ourselves, because in the midst of our ignorance we often lose sight of God. It is then that our fears are magnified. So David asks, "Soul, why are you agitated like waves on a stormy sea?" It is as if he says to himself, "What's wrong with you? Stop looking at the storm and start looking at God—hope in God. And when you do focus on Him, your spirits will be lifted up and you will say, 'I shall yet praise Him.'"

The phrase "For the help of His countenance" is literally "for the salvation of His face." In other words he looks forward to when he would recognize God's presence in his situation and His sustaining grace and help in it. It is similar to the hope of disheartened believers today who turn their eyes away from circumstances to "consider Him who endured such hostility from sinners against Himself" (Heb. 12:3). Reminding ourselves of how Christ endured what He did lends both a spiritual and an eternal perspective to our problems.

God Is My Sure Hope (42:6-11)

"My soul is cast down within me" (42:6)

Hoping in God is more than desire that everything will turn out all right in the end. The concept of *hope* in the Bible is one of full confidence that is founded in God's unchanging character and in His promises. The second section of this psalm, like the first, starts with a lament and ends with hope. David's despondency has returned in the second cycle, but again his faith fights back based on the promise of God. Many believers battle depression from time to time, but the wise ones are those who have learned that fighting back by exercising faith in God's promises is the key to victory over it. In his second cycle, David begins, "O my God, my soul is cast down within me." The words "cast down" mean to sink down. The metaphor changes from a deer panting for a drink of water to a drowning man being swallowed up by water. He speaks of the Jordan River and its sources in the heights of Mount Hermon. The location of Mizar is unknown.

"All Your billows and waves have gone over me" (42:7)

David sees his soul as if it were caught in a pool below a waterfall. His hope fades as he finds himself trapped in the currents caused by the waterfall. Jonah the prophet quoted this psalm when he was in the ocean within the belly of the great fish. He described his suffering using the psalmist's words, "All Your billows and Your waves passed over me" (Jonah 2:3). The hymn writer H. G. Spafford lost four daughters at one time when their ship went down in the Atlantic. In his well-known hymn he referred to this tragedy with words from this psalm, "When sorrows like sea billows roll," but he went on to declare, "Whatever my lot, Thou hast taught me to say, 'It is well, it is well with my soul.'"

David is like that hymn writer. Even with his depressed condition pulling him down, his mind turns back to the loving-kindness of the Lord.

Notice those two words. Both the words "loving-kindness" and "Lord" are closely connected with the covenant promises of God to Israel. The psalmist clings to them (v. 7).

"A prayer to the God of my life" (42:8)

Notice that both "in the daytime" and "in the night" David is conscious that he can claim God's promise and sing God's song because God is the God of his life. God created life and sustains life. Notice also that here we have the answer to the tears in verse 3. In that verse, his tears were his food day and night. Now in verse 8 his cries of despair have changed to a song of joy. This is the way of victory for us who are sinking down in the deep waters of despair. Claim the promises of a God who made a covenant to bless His people. Then sing God's song day and night and speak in prayer to the God of your life.

David Questions God (42:9)

The psalmist goes on to explain his feelings to God. He reminds himself that God is his rock, the one who provides security, stability, and strength. He is the one who never changes. So he can say in effect: "I will take my stand on You, my Rock." Then he asks himself, "Why do I allow myself to think that You have forgotten me? Why do I mourn when the enemy opposes me? Why do I even entertain the thought that God is so un-rocklike that He would forget His servant?" And beyond that he is asking God the Rock to restore his security and strength.

We often ask God why He seems to be so far away. And just as often there seems to be no immediate answer. But even when that happens, our humble asking prepares us to praise Him for His answer when it becomes clear. It is also comforting to know that the way of the Lord is perfect, that is, complete. He designs everything surrounding us for our ultimate good and for His glory.

David's Enemies Question Him (42:10)

The psalmist is also aware that, whatever the divine purpose of his suffering, his enemies may take advantage of it and add to it by jeering at him and taunting him (v. 10). Their mocking pains him deeply. One of Satan's favorite sword-like "thrusts" is to taunt suffering believers by asking where God is in the midst of trials. He implies that God has forsaken you in your moment of need, or on the other hand that you deserve what you have received because you have been unfaithful to Him. It is a cruel thrust, because neither of those options may be the truth. When we are plagued with such thoughts, we must turn back to God's Word for assurance of His promises and for light to discern any sin on our part.

"Hope in God" (42:11)

The psalmist is aware of the tactics of the enemy. Instead of answering the enemy, he lectures his own soul once again, just as he did in verse 5. "Why are you cast down, O my soul? And why are you disquieted within me?" He does not concentrate on the hurt caused by his enemies, nor does he doubt God's goodness in allowing him to endure the trials. Instead he gives himself a lecture, saying something like, "Soul, think about it! If God is on the throne, you really don't have grounds for being cast down."

> True faith sees the goodness of God in every circumstance.

He goes on to say to his soul, "Hope in God; for I shall yet praise Him." True faith sees the goodness of God in every circumstance. The phrase "My hope is in the Lord" appears eleven times in the book of Psalms. The section ends with the phrase, "The help of my countenance and my God." It is slightly different from the parallel phrase in verse 5 where it says, "The help of *His* countenance." Here it is *my* countenance, which indicates that when the psalmist hopes in God, his own face would be made to shine. So don't doubt Him. Don't blame Him. David then adds "And my God," which answers the question of his enemies in verse 10, "Where is your God?" God *is* near, and He acts for the blessing of His people.

God Is My Just Hope (43:1-5)

"Vindicate me, O God" (43:1)

The third section is structured just like the previous two (Ps. 42:1-5, 6-11). All three end with the same self-directed lecture. David may have written this psalm some time later than Psalm 42 when he had meditated further on the subject—even though circumstances had not yet changed.

Thus he adds a third section. God is the answer to the psalmist's dilemma in all three: (1) God is the water for which the thirsty deer longs (42:1-5); (2) God is the rock for which for which the troubled soul longs (42:6-11); and (3) God is the judge for whom the one who is falsely accused longs (43:1-5).

The imagery in Psalm 43 is a courtroom scene. It begins with the psalmist as the accused saying "Vindicate me, O God, and plead my cause against an ungodly nation." David wants his cause brought before God, who he knows will judge him impartially. His enemies are deceitful and unjust, and God alone has the power to deliver him from their evil intentions. In addition, God alone has the authority to exact vengeance on them, because vengeance belongs to Him. It is tempting for believers to take things into their own hands and exact the due penalty to "get even" with those who have injured them, but God says, "Vengeance is Mine, I will repay" (Rom. 12:19). Thus it is in God's hands to deliver the unjustly treated believer and to repay the perpetrator for unjust treatment.

"You are the God of my strength" (43:2)

The psalmist then explains why God should answer his prayer—because "You are the God of my strength." All my strength comes from God, and therefore I leave the task of combating my foes entirely in His hands. We are blessed if we learn that truth early in life. David has given God solid reasons why he should be delivered from evil and why his enemies should be punished. And so he launches into his third lament that God has not yet seen fit to deliver him or to judge his enemies. He says, "Why do You cast me off?" It is as if to say, "Why do I wander all over the country mourning and grieving with my enemy still pursuing me?" When we are speaking to God like this we must be careful not to question His motives. It is better to humbly yield to the things we do not understand. However, candid questions like this show how approachable God is; we should therefore feel free to express ourselves openly to Him when we are hurting.

"Send out Your light and Your truth!" (43:3)

The psalmist then humbly asks that God, as Light, would show him the way forward, and that God, as Truth, would assure him it was the right way. Light and truth are both symbols of God's Word. In Psalm 119 the writer says, "Your Word is a lamp to my feet" and 'Your law is truth" (vv.

105 and 142). God guides us with the light of His Word; then He assures us with the truth of His Word. Thus with the psalmist we can say, "Let them lead me."

"I shall yet praise Him" (43:4-5)

David prays that God's light and truth will bring him to the "holy hill," another term for the tabernacle. Then for the third and final time David challenges his own soul not to be disquieted with unreasonable fears. He again exhorts his soul to hope in God, that is, to wait for God. He would try to focus on God, not his circumstances. Then his countenance, or face, would shine with the light of God's presence and glory.

Looking back over the three sections of these two psalms, when we "hope in God," three wonderful things happen: our thirst for Him is quenched by the Living Water; our need for stability is provided by the immovable Rock; and our accusers in court are silenced by God the Judge of all the earth.

7

PSALM 46
THE LORD IS OUR SECURE REFUGE

Psalm 46 is the first of three psalms sometimes called "the Songs of Zion." They all celebrate the deliverance of Jerusalem from her enemies and the establishment of God's presence there. In Psalm 46, God is present as a refuge for His people. In Psalm 47, He is present as the King of all the earth on His throne. And in Psalm 48, He is present as the King who is Victor over all His enemies.

> God is present
> as a refuge for
> His people.

The title of Psalm 46 indicates its place in the praise music associated with the temple. It was written "to the Chief Musician," who directed the singing. It was a psalm of the "sons of Korah," who were the practicing temple musicians. And it was "a Song for Alamoth," probably indicating the leading soprano voices of the young women who sang and danced in praise to God after victories. Examples of women praising God in song in the Old Testament include those led by Miriam after Pharaoh's army was drowned in the Red Sea (Ex. 15:20-21) and the women who sang and danced after David's victory over Goliath (1 Sam. 18:6-7).

Historical Background

Many commentators think that this psalm was inspired by the victory of Hezekiah, king of Judah, over the Assyrian army in 701 BC. Nearly twenty years earlier, the Assyrian king Sargon II had defeated the northern kingdom of Israel, destroyed its capital (Samaria), and deported the people into exile. Sargon's son, Sennacherib, then invaded the southern kingdom of Judah and took city after city throughout the land. He first demanded that King Hezekiah pay heavy tribute in exchange for peace. Hezekiah did so, but later Sennacherib also demanded Jerusalem's surrender. Hezekiah refused, so Sennacherib and his vast army besieged Jerusalem. They publicly mocked the God of Israel, but King Hezekiah and Isaiah the prophet put their trust in God. They prayed, "O Lord of hosts . . . save us from his hand, that all the kingdoms of the earth may know that You are the Lord, You alone" (Isa. 37:16-20). The "Lord of hosts" *did* deliver them. That very night an angel of the Lord killed 185,000 Assyrian soldiers who were surrounding Jerusalem, and the battle was over (Isa. 37:36-37).

Psalm 46 was most likely written to celebrate the victory and the presence of the Lord of Hosts in Jerusalem as the refuge for His people. Twice the theme is stated, "The Lord of hosts is with us; The God of Jacob is our refuge" (vv. 7, 11). Hezekiah himself may have been the author. He observed that when the enemy seemed unbeatable, God intervened and protected Jerusalem and its people. It is not surprising therefore, that when God's people today find themselves in disastrous circumstances, this is the psalm they often turn to for encouragement.

God Is Our Refuge (vv. 1-3)

"God is our refuge" (v. 1)

A refuge is a place to go for protection when disaster seems imminent. In ancient times, cities were built as stone-walled fortresses to serve as a refuge for their inhabitants. Their modern equivalent would

> We have a refuge and stronghold— none other than God Himself.

be tornado shelters. Hikers may find refuge from a storm in a mountain cave. Ships will find refuge in a harbor to gain safety from a threatening storm. God's people are threatened by other kinds of attacks from which they need refuge. These attacks come in many forms and are designed by our enemy, Satan, to hinder our usefulness to God and our enjoying the spiritual blessings God has provided us in Christ. The most damaging attacks strike our minds and emotions. When they strike, we have a refuge and stronghold—not a physical place, but a person: none other than God Himself.

"God is our . . . strength" (v. 1)

In addition to God being our refuge in whom we can find protection from our enemies, He is also our inner strength in whom we can find provision (or, enabling power) to face our failures and fears with courage and confidence. The prophet Jeremiah spoke of the righteous finding God as their refuge from attack (Jer. 17:17). In Psalm 18:2 David claimed God was his fortress and his stronghold. The writer of Hebrews speaks of Jesus as the refuge to whom believers have fled for eternal security (Heb. 6:18).

God is also a "very present help in trouble." The word "trouble" means literally "in tight places" and implies stress and distress from situations we find ourselves in. God is immediately at hand when the pressure increases. We are assured of His availability whenever we need Him.

"Therefore we will not fear" (vv. 2-3)

With God as our refuge and strength, the psalmist's conclusion is a strong declaration: "we will not fear." The people in Jerusalem under siege were safe even though they were surrounded by the Assyrian army, because God was their refuge. And we today who have taken refuge in God as our fortress are

—— ❧ ——

"If God is for us, who can be against us?"
–Romans 8:31

—— ❧ ——

perfectly safe from anything that the enemy might hurl against us. In New Testament times, Paul echoed this same truth to the Christians in Rome when he declared, "If God is for us, who can be against us?" (Rom. 8:31).

The psalmist illustrates how safe the fortress is by imagining the strongest known physical force that might be thrown against it: a terrible earthquake that causes the entire configuration of the earth to be changed and mountains to be moved into the sea, which in turn causes the sea to rise like a tsunami (vv. 2-3). Being local to such a catastrophe would strike fear in any person's heart. God is our fortress, and His gates are secure; all His people are safe inside. At this point the psalmist says, "Selah." He speaks to those in the choir, and to you and me as well. It means, "Take a breath and think about those who are safe in the fortress. Terrible wars may shake and change the world, pride may swell up like a tsunami wave, but those in the fortress are all safe. God is our refuge."

God Is Our Provider (vv. 4-7)

"There is a river" (v. 4)

In this second section, the imagery changes to a scene inside the city of God, a scene of great peace and tranquility. A river flows through this city, and the citizens enjoy the life, beauty, and refreshment it provides. This scene is set in contrast to the trembling earth and wild waves pounding on the walls of the fortress.

Hezekiah's Tunnel

In the historical record, King Hezekiah had concluded that the Assyrian army was coming and would besiege the city of Jerusalem. During any siege, water is the most important element for the survival of those inside. Jerusalem had a large and dependable spring called Sihon near the wall on the eastern side. A channel ran from the spring outside the wall for four hundred yards south and then back inside the wall to the pool of Siloam. Hezekiah knew this was vulnerable, so he had a 1,777 feet-long tunnel built through solid rock from the spring to the pool (2 Kings 20:20). He then covered the spring with rock, completely hiding it from the enemy. The result was that all during the siege there existed a river that brought an unending water supply into the city. In the poetic terms of this psalm, it "made glad the city of God." It was a hidden source of life within the city, and unknown to the enemy.

In the Bible, rivers are often used to describe conditions of peace.

Isaiah the prophet was living in Jerusalem at the time Hezekiah was king. It is therefore no surprise that if Hezekiah wrote this psalm, he would use similar expressions to those of Isaiah. In his great prophecy, Isaiah compared the Assyrian army to a strong and mighty river that almost engulfed Judah. Then he contrasted this wild river with the peaceful flow of water from the spring into the Pool of Siloam (Isa. 8:6-7). The psalmist uses similar imagery of the roaring waves against the walls of the city contrasted with the peaceful stream that brings life and refreshment. In the Bible, rivers are often used to describe conditions of peace, the last of which is a river in the eternal heavenly city (Rev. 22:1).

"God is in the midst of her" (v. 5)

The spiritual lesson for us here is that the supply of God's grace is sufficient for His people even though they are surrounded by spiritual enemies. God dwells with His people now, just as He did in the ancient city of Jerusalem. The refreshment He brings through His Spirit makes us glad. In addition to supplying daily grace, He protects His people; therefore, Zion (and we) will not be moved (cf. Ps. 10:6, 30:6). Zion cannot fall because God is within her. So the psalmist exults, "God shall help her, just at the break of dawn" (v. 5). That is exactly what happened! The besieging enemy was poised to capture the city at dawn, but God sent an angel through the enemy camp and destroyed the advancing army before they could mount their attack.

A Strong Enemy is Overthrown (v. 6)

The psalmist returns to his vision of the fury of the enemies of God's people (vv. 2-3). The word in verse 6 for "raged" is the same as the word for "roar" in verse 3. The word for "moved" is the same as the word for "carried" in verse 2. In Hebrew there are seven words used here to describe the whole power of the enemies surrounding the city of God: "The nations raged, the kingdoms were moved." Then God decisively intervened on behalf of His people, and seven further words are used to describe the complete overthrow of the enemy: "He uttered His voice, the earth melted" (v. 6). When God's voice commanded His angel to destroy them, the proud army of the Assyrians melted like wax in the morning sun. Their fury was all to no avail because God was fighting for His people.

"The LORD of Hosts is with us" (v. 7)

God is identified as the "LORD of hosts." One solitary angel was sufficient to destroy the Assyrian army. The Lord who was "with" His people in Jerusalem was also the commander of uncounted hosts of angels. Isaiah uses the title "LORD of hosts" frequently to remind the people of His power, beginning in Isaiah 1:9. The psalmist also calls Him the "God of Jacob," a name that reminds us that He was always Jacob's refuge. This is comforting, because Jacob was a man who failed frequently. And it was the same with the people whose nation was named after Jacob. They failed too, but God was a refuge to them. And for us who also fail, He is *our* refuge.

Added to the comfort of knowing that God is "the LORD of hosts" and that He is willing to be termed "the God of Jacob" is the assurance that "God is with us." The Hebrew word "with us" is *immanu,* from which we get the messianic title, Immanuel—"God with us." In effect, the battle for Jerusalem was won before the Assyrian army ever left Ninevah, their capital. The application of this truth for us as believers is that the Lord Jesus has come to take up residence in our hearts and lives in us through His Spirit. He is Emmanuel, "God with us" (Matt. 1:23), He is with us as the Lord of hosts, our Victor. He is also with us as the God of Jacob, our restoration from our failures. The section aptly closes with the refrain, "Selah"—stop and think about that!

The Lord Is Our Peacemaker (vv. 8-11)

"Come, behold the works of the LORD" (vv. 8-9)

In the final section, the residents of Jerusalem are counseled to be wise by considering (weighing up) the works of God. They were to go and see the field of battle outside Jerusalem. It was strewn with the remains of their enemies that gave witness to the works of the Lord. His works brought desolation to their enemies, but in so doing they also brought peace to His people. Spurgeon advises us to apply the truth of this verse to all the ruins of wars in history. In doing so, we see that God makes desolations in the earth in the process of implementing His program for the world and His care for His own people. What He did in Jerusalem in 701 BC has been repeated many times. The desolate ruins of Tyre, Babylon, Nineveh, Jericho, Petra, Baashan, Athens, and Rome all testify to the hand of God in shaping history for His purpose and glory. "Come, behold the works of the LORD."

The desolations that God inflicts on His enemies are the prelude to the victories and blessing He will bestow on the righteous in the future. This passage is eschatological—it prophesies what will take place in the future when the earth is desolate, when few men are left, when the earth is violently broken, when the earth is shaken exceedingly (Isa. 24:6, 19). This is the time when the kings of the earth will gather at Armageddon to make war against Christ (Rev. 19:19). They will be destroyed by the desolations and "He [will make] wars cease to the end of the earth" (v. 9). Then He will break the weapons of war (Isa. 2:4; Micah 4:3). The Lord will speak peace to the nations. His dominion will be from sea to sea (Zech. 9:10) and the earth shall be filled with the knowledge of the Lord as the waters cover the sea.

"Be still, and know that I am God" (vv. 10-11)

We have considered the application to the past when the Lord defeated the Assyrians that besieged Jerusalem. We have considered the future when the Lord will come and fight against the nations who will attack His people in Jerusalem during the campaign of Armageddon. Now let us look at these verses with a view to the present. As believers today, we too may be surrounded and threatened by enemies of God, but the "The LORD of hosts is with us; The God of Jacob is our refuge" (v. 11).

God speaks as the guarantor of both personal peace and universal peace. He says, "Be still, and know that I am God." It was His voice that overthrew the Assyrians in the days of Hezekiah (v. 6). It is His voice that silences our rising fears and encourages us along the way. In the final scene with the new heaven and the new earth we are reminded of John's vision. He "heard a loud voice from heaven saying, 'Behold, the tabernacle of God is with men, and He will dwell with them, and they shall be His people. God Himself will be with them and be their God'" (Rev. 21:3).

The Voice says to us, "Be still, and know that I am God." The normal way for God to carry on His work is to use people. But sometimes God tells us simply to be still so that we can remember who He is, letting Him do the work. He does it in His own way without us. It is good for us sometimes to stand still and wait patiently for the Lord. As we watch, we will see the mighty hand of God doing His work. God is not advising us to give ourselves to nothing but contemplation, but to stop our fruitless self-effort and surrender to Him. In particular, we should not fear (cf. v. 2). Then we will acknowledge that He is the one and only victorious God. Isaiah said it like this: "In quietness and confidence shall be your strength" (Isa. 30:15)

The LORD of Hosts

The title "LORD of hosts" appears here for the second time (cf. v. 7). As we have seen, the "hosts" probably referred in the immediate context to the angelic hosts of heaven who protected the residents of Jerusalem. The link between this name for God and the deliverance of Jerusalem in Hezekiah's day is once again in view. Prophetically it looks forward to the final deliverance of His people from all their foes at the end of the tribulation when the Lord comes to set up His kingdom in that city. In our daily lives we have this same Lord of hosts with us.

In the final verse we are reminded again that the mighty Lord of hosts is also the God of Jacob, the covenant-keeping God of those who are weak and fallible, like Jacob. He is with us. John Wesley's last words as he was dying were, "And best of all, God is with us." Selah!

8

PSALM 63
THE LORD IS MY ONLY
SOURCE OF CONTENTMENT

Psalm 63 is one of general psalms in which the writer expresses the satisfaction he has found in his relationship with God despite his earthly circumstances. He therefore pours out his heart to God from the depths of his emotions and spiritual longing. His exercise of soul and spirit has struck a chord in many of God's people down through history.

Historical Background

The title tells us that the psalmist is David and that he wrote it while in the wilderness of Judah. There were two periods in David's life when he lived in such conditions. As the psalm refers to him being king (v. 11), it must relate to the time when his son Absalom led a rebellion against him and usurped his throne. In an effort to divert Absalom from attacking Jerusalem, David fled from the city. He and some loyal followers traveled through the wilderness of Judah and across the Jordan River (2 Samuel 15). Absalom could easily have defeated and killed David at that point, but instead he took the advice of counselors and delayed pursuing him. By the time they met in battle, David had organized his army and the rebels were defeated, losing 20,000 men—Absalom among them.

A Song of Devotion

David wrote this psalm during his short exile in the wilderness while his life was under threat, but these dangers did not paralyze him with fear. Instead he responded with devotion to God. What he longed for was not so much personal security as closeness to God. Thus the psalm consists in an outpouring of his love for God. It resembles a love song—David the "lover" longs for his "beloved," God, from whom he feels separated.

We who are God's people today live in a "wilderness" world, and there is a usurper on the throne—Satan. But although we live in this wilderness we can sing songs of worship to Him who will soon come and establish His own power and glory in the world. Our souls can enjoy intimacy with God despite our surroundings, just as David's soul did. David refers to his soul three times in Psalm 63. In verse 1 he says, "My soul thirsts for You." In verse 5 he says, "My soul shall be satisfied." And in verse 8 he says, "My soul follows close behind You." Using these as our outline we shall note (1) David's soul thirsting for God while in the wilderness (vv. 1-4); (2) David's soul satisfied with God in the night (vv. 5-7); and (3) David's soul clinging to God in the presence of his enemies (vv. 8-11).

David's Soul Thirsts for God (vv. 1-4)

David Thirsts for God Himself (vv. 1-2)

David begins by addressing God as "my God," claiming his personal relationship with Him as the reason why God should attend closely to his prayer. David does not use the name Yahweh (the God who keeps covenant) but Elohim, God the Almighty Creator to whom nothing is impossible. In addressing Him as his God it is as if he is saying, "You, Elohim, in all the fullness of Your infinite resources, in all Your power and glory, You are my God."

David then prays, "Early will I seek You." Literally this means, "With the breaking in of the morning I will seek You." Bible translations render it in two ways.

> David sets us the example of spending time with God both *early* and *earnestly*.

Some, like the NKJV, translate it as seeking God "early"; others, like the NASB, translate it as seeking God "earnestly." Both ideas are instructive, for David sets us the example of spending time with God both *early* and *earnestly*. When we seek Him early in the day, we express the priority we are giving Him in our lives. When we seek Him earnestly, we convey that we seriously want to benefit from His instruction and guidance.

David was an exile in the wilderness, which he calls "a dry and thirsty land." He used that background of being physically thirsty away from the abundance of his palace to illustrate how His soul was spiritually thirsty for God away from the sanctuary (the tabernacle). Just as water is indispensable for life, so God is indispensable for his soul. We must remember that the tabernacle represented God's presence among His people and His favor towards them. David, as a devoted believer in Yahweh, was keenly aware of that. David's thirst was therefore an intense desire for God's presence.

Verse 2 seems to be connected with the early hours of David's flight from Absalom (2 Samuel 15). David noticed that Zadok the high priest had joined those escaping with him and that other priests were bringing with them the Ark of the Covenant, no doubt thinking that keeping the Ark with David would guarantee God's presence and, therefore, David's safety. But when David saw them carrying it he told them to return it to Jerusalem saying, "If I find favor in the eyes of the LORD, He will bring me back and show me both it and His dwelling place." David wanted God's presence more than anything else, but he knew enough to know that he needed God Himself, not the Ark, which was but the *symbol* of His presence (2 Sam. 15:24-25). In his commentary on the Psalms, Derek Kidner says that "God is not the prisoner of His sanctuary." David believed that he could (and would) witness God's power and glory in the barren wilderness just as he did when worshiping Him at His earthly sanctuary, the tabernacle. We too should learn that we can enter into God's presence to praise Him and to pray to Him no matter our circumstances or location.

David Praises God's Loving-kindness (v. 3)

When David was fleeing from Jerusalem, his life was in grave danger. Most people will do almost anything to preserve their lives, but to David there was something far more precious than his life. It was God's loving-kindness—a word that includes His attributes of His grace, love, mercy, and faithfulness. It is sometimes translated "covenant love" or "steadfast love," the idea being that God's love continues forever towards His own people. His love is "better than [earthly] life" in that it outlasts it. Paul conveyed this to the Roman believers when he posed the question, "Who shall separate us from the love of Christ?" He answered it by stating that nothing in heaven, earth, life, or death, can separate us from the love of God because we are now in Christ (Rom. 8:35-39). When David recalled the power and glory of God and meditated on His loving-kindness, he seemed to forget his difficult surroundings. Such is the experience of all who focus their hearts and minds on the person of God and the spiritual blessings He showers on us.

David couldn't hold back from declaring his praise verbally. He wanted everyone else to know of God's love too. His attitude reminds us of the four lepers in the days of Elisha the prophet (much later in Israel's history). Their city of Samaria was being besieged by the armies of Syria (2 Kings 6-7). They and the city's residents were in desperate need of food. Then one night God caused the Syrian troops to hear the sound of a great army approaching, causing them to panic and flee and to leave their tents and all their provisions behind. At the same time, the lepers decided that they would go and beg from the attacking army—they figured that they had nothing to lose. To their great surprise they found the camp deserted. They ate and drank their fill and then came to their senses, saying to one other, "We are not doing right. This day is a day of good news, and we remain silent . . . . Let us go and tell the king's household" (2 Kings 7:9). As a result of sharing the good news, sacks of flour and barley were selling cheaply in Samaria within one day. The obvious lesson for us is that we should not keep the fact of God's loving-kindness to ourselves; we should share it with others so that they too may benefit from God's provision.

David Determines to Live for God's Glory (v. 4)

As David blessed the Lord in worship, he lifted up his hands to Him. This biblical gesture indicated a posture of prayer (Ps. 28:2; Lam. 2:19) and of respect (Ps. 119:48). In 1 Timothy 2:8 the apostle Paul exhorts that men pray "lifting up holy hands," implying they should come into God's presence with nothing to hide, having confessed all known sin. Note that the word "Thus" at the beginning of verse 4 connects it with verse 3. David's response to God's love for him was praise and prayer. The phrase "while I live" is literally "in my life." It means both "as long as I live" and "with all the power of my life." So David determined to bless God for the duration of his life and *with* his life. He purposed to live his life giving honor to the Lord in everything. Paul summarized the purpose of his life with the statement, "To me to live is Christ" (Phil. 1:21).

David's Soul is Satisfied by God (vv. 5-7)

To explain how satisfied he was now, David used the illustration of God as the host of a banquet at which he was the guest. The table would be loaded with the richest and choicest of foods. This is what he means by the terms "marrow and fatness." The guests enjoy the food and compliment their host for the wonderful things He has provided. They praise Him with joyful lips, that is, with song (v. 5). They are delighted with His generosity and they sing His praise. Thus David, having enjoyed God's banquet table, can lie down to rest, fully satisfied.

David now reveals the true secret of his satisfaction. He had been king for many years, but he was currently a fugitive. In the palace he would have regularly enjoyed sumptuous banquet fare, but now he and his friends had only meager trail food to share. It wasn't banquet food that brought him satisfaction, however—it was God who satisfied him. In Old Testament times, the night was divided into three watches of four hours each (cf. Judges 7:19). When David lay awake during the night, he would meditate on the nature of his God, especially His power to protect (v. 7). So in the dark of the night, instead of being afraid that his enemies might attack and capture him, and instead of thinking back to the great banquets at the palace table, he meditated on God.

Perhaps you find it hard to sleep when you are going through trials. Follow David's example of meditating on God and the way He has cared for you in the past. When you do that, those wakeful hours in the dark of night that often seem to magnify the problems we face will become times of spiritual profit and rest for your soul.

When David did this, his faith grew stronger. He remembered that God had been his help, even from his youth (v. 7). He remembered that God had kept His promise to make him king and had sustained him through the long years of being a fugitive from Saul. Therefore, why should he not believe, even now, that God would bring him through this trial? Beyond that, God had made covenant promises concerning the future of his dynasty that He would certainly fulfill (1 Sam. 7:8-17). God had promised that David's name, nation, throne, and kingdom would last forever when the Messiah, the greater David would come. If all that was true, then would not God bring him through this temporary setback? David could be as safe, happy, and secure as a young bird under the shadow of its mother's wings. (v. 7, cf. Ps. 17:8). The apostle Paul argued in the same way that God who had delivered him out of the mouth of the lion would also deliver him and preserve him for His heavenly kingdom (2 Tim. 4:17). Because God had been David's help, David could say, "I will rejoice" (v. 7).

David's Soul Clings to God (vv. 8-11)

David Commits to God's Leadership (v. 8)

The final section of Psalm 63 concludes with David *clinging to God in the presence of his enemies*. Note the order here. First his thirst for God was quenched. This made him satisfied with God so that he sang for joy. Now he clings to God, even though surrounded by enemies.

Verse 8 begins "My soul follows close behind You." The phrase "follows close behind" is translated "clings" in the NASB, and "stay close" in the NIV. The same word is used four times in the story of Ruth (1:14, 2:8, 21, and 23). In that story, three sad widows were about to part from each other. Naomi had been living in Moab, away from her God, her people, and her land. She had lost her husband and now just wanted to live out her days back home in Bethlehem. Although her daughter-in-law Orpah decided to return to Moab, Naomi's other daughter-in-law, Ruth, "clung" to Naomi. Ruth then explained how she would "cling" to Naomi:

> **The person who clings to God is, at the same time, upheld by God.**

"Entreat me not to leave you, or to turn back from following after you; for wherever you go, I will go; and wherever you lodge, I will lodge; Your people shall be my people, and your God, my God." So David says to God, "My soul follows hard after You."

Following after God was one of the things that Moses taught Israel. In his farewell address to them he reminded them five times that they were to "hold fast" to God along with loving Him, fearing Him, and obeying Him (Deut. 4:4, 10:20, 11:22, 13:4, and 30:20).

We should note an important point here. Holding fast is only half of the story. Verse 8 also says, "Your right hand upholds me." There is a wonderful balance here. The person who clings to God is, at the same time, upheld by God. Imagine a father walking hand-in-hand with his young son. When his son senses danger, he holds on tightly to his father's hand. That is what it means to cling. But at the same time as the boy grips his father, his father is holding him securely. The child is as safe as he could be. When my own son Peter was about four-years-old, we were walking through a tunnel in a dam used for the city water system of Durban, South Africa. It was pitch black, and Peter held my hand tightly while I kept his firmly in mine. He said to me in the dark, "Daddy, if you hold my hand, I could go anywhere." David felt the same way with God holding his hand. We should be conscious that God holds our hand and we are therefore safe.

David Trusts in God's Justice (vv. 9-11)

From the place of his own security David is aware that his enemies are seeking to destroy him, but he confidently asserts their destruction. Rather than becoming overly-occupied with any vindictive element here on David's part, it is better to view the overall tone as one of his confidence in God to preserve him and to deal justly with his enemies. This is a perspective that we can all apply to ourselves. We too can have confidence that God will take care of us and judge the enemies of our soul in His time and way.

> God will judge the ungodly according to His own timetable.

Not only will God's justice triumph over David's enemies at last, but he will be restored as the king of Israel. His faith in God returning him to Jerusalem to resume his reign is evidenced by his referring to himself here as "the king." He anticipates rejoicing in God when this event takes place. And all those who have sworn allegiance to God (and to His anointed king) shall "glory." That is, they will boast their victory over their enemies, whose mouths will have been stopped. The smear campaign that Absalom had waged to obtain power would be stopped. In David's case, all the lies and hatred that Shimei had poured out on him would end (in fact, Shimei would soon plead for David's forgiveness—read 2 Samuel 16-19).

David sets us an example to exercise faith in God by reminding ourselves of His justice in relation to both the righteous and the ungodly. He will vindicate whatever injustices we, the righteous, may suffer for His sake, and He will judge the ungodly according to His own timetable. These truths should help us endure injustice and to genuinely rejoice in God and find our full satisfaction in Him.

9

PSALM 90
THE LORD IS OUR ETERNAL
DWELLING PLACE

The title attributes Psalm 90 to Moses the "man of God," a title
given to him in Deuteronomy 33:1. (It is a title reserved for only a
few others in Scripture. These include Samuel, David, Elijah, Elisha, and
Timothy.) This psalm is the only one attributed to Moses, although Psalm
91 is also reckoned by some scholars to be written by him, partly because
it has no superscription. The Bible contains two other songs authored by
Moses. One was a song of praise and thanksgiving after he had led the
Israelites across the Red Sea (Ex. 15:1-18). The other was at the conclusion
of his farewell address to the Israelites just before he died at age 120 (Deut.
32:1-43).

Historical Background

Moses had always had a strong sense of God's glory and holiness. Think
of God's revelation to him at the burning bush and God's power displayed
in the ten plagues. Think of the glory he saw in the glowing pillar of cloud
and in the parting of the Red Sea. Think of the terror of the Lord he had
experienced in being in the glory-cloud on Mount Sinai when he heard the
voice of God in giving the law. Think of the awe produced in him at the
miraculous provision of food and water in the wilderness, and of victory in
battle when all the odds were against them, or of the plagues and judgments
God meted out to the Israelites who rebelled against Him.

For the most part, Moses not only had a strong sense of God's glory,
but of his own frailty. The one time that we know he drew attention away

from God's glory and onto himself, he and Aaron were judged unfit to take the people into the Promised Land. He was thus reminded of God's holy character in a way that affected him personally. Read of this incident in Numbers 20:1-12. This psalm was probably written as a result of this incident, which occurred near the end of the Israelites' forty-year period of God-ordained wandering in the wilderness and soon after Miriam, Moses' sister, died. Of all the Israelite adults who left Egypt, Joshua and Caleb were the only ones to enter the Promised Land.

As we meditate on this psalm we gain an eternal perspective of God. We learn to number (make the most of) our days in light of God's eternality and immutability. While everything around changes and the cycles of life and death continue, the one constant is our unchanging God.

Structure

Psalm 90 addresses the frailty and brevity of human life compared with the eternal character of God. But in the psalm Moses shows no sign of despair in relation to the prospect of his own passing or that of his siblings'. Instead, he writes with a meek and submissive spirit. It is a national psalm relating to Israel. It is not written from a personal perspective, though personal applications may be made from it. The psalm has five sections; note the flow of thought.

➢ The Lord is our eternal dwelling place (vv. 1-2).

➢ God's eternal existence is contrasted with our brief life on earth (vv. 3-6).

➢ The brevity of human life is linked to God's righteous anger against sin (vv. 7-10).

➢ God's anger against sin leads to a prayer for a heart of wisdom (vv. 11-12).

➢ With wisdom we pray for God's mercy and favor on us and our activities (vv. 13-17).

God's Eternal and Permanent Nature (vv. 1-2)

Moses acknowledges that God had always been Israel's dwelling-place. The Israelites had left their homes in Egypt forty years before and had their hopes fixed on future homes in Canaan. During their journey in the wilderness they had been nomads. They were pilgrims on their way to a better land. Nothing around them was permanent. But Moses had the spiritual perception to see that the true dwelling place of God's people was not on earth, but in God Himself. We too need to learn that in the world there is no specific place we can truly call "home." Our true home of rest, security, and refuge is in a person—God. And this home, like that of Israel, is not limited to our own generation, but was and is for all generations.

> Our true home of rest, security, and refuge is in God.

By the time Moses wrote this psalm he would probably have written the Pentateuch (the first five books of the Bible), in which he recorded God's dealings with many generations back to Adam. He knew well that God had been his people's dwelling place through all the generations of history. God had been there in the Garden of Eden with Adam and Eve. He had been there in the ark with Noah during the flood and with Abram on his journey to Canaan. He had been in Canaan with Jacob, and in Pharaoh's court with Joseph. The word "dwelling place" is translated "refuge" in other places. The word indicates a safe and secure place. Our security is forever because God's everlasting arms hold us (Deut. 33:27). Have you discovered that the world is not your home and that God is your dwelling place and your refuge? How wonderful that when we are in the family of God we are already safe at home with God!

> How wonderful that when we are in the family of God we are already safe at home with God!

Verse 2 tells us that God existed before the foundation of the world. Mountains are called "everlasting hills" here and are used in the Bible as a symbol of strength, but God existed before them. He is before creation and apart from creation. From the everlasting past to the everlasting future, He was, is, and will be. No doubt Moses recalled the incident at the burning bush when God told him that He was the "I Am," the self-existent One (Exodus 3).

Man's Brief and Temporary Life (v. 3-6)

Moses now contrasts the eternality of God with the brevity of human life. First Moses says "Return, O children of men," that is, to dust. Adam, the first man, was created by God from dust (cf. Gen. 2:7 and 3:19), and we, Adam's descendants, return to dust when He determines we will die.

How true it is that our times are in God's hands, and they are very brief at that. But even if a man lives a thousand years—and many of the ancients did live nearly that long—man's life on earth is like yesterday that is past, just one day. Compared to eternity, our lives are short. Man's short life is like one four-hour watch in the nighttime. It passes, and we are not aware of it because we are sleeping (v. 4). So we are to grasp the contrast between the brief life of man and the eternal existence of the changeless, ageless Creator. Peter, in New Testament times, quotes this verse to remind us that while we wait anxiously for the Lord's return, God is not slow in bringing it about (2 Peter 3:8).

Man's brevity of life is now compared to the things that are swept away just like a flood sweeps everything before it without warning (v. 5). It is also like the desert grass that grows in the morning after a rain but which quickly fades and withers in the scorching heat of the sun that follows it (v. 6). Thus man's life on earth is short, his end comes quickly, and his end usually means destruction.

God's Righteous Anger Against Sin (vv. 7-8)

Moses has been reflecting on the brevity of man's life on earth in view of the fact that a whole generation of Israelites had died during their forty years in the wilderness. Now Moses speaks more specifically about the Israelites during that time. They died in the wilderness because they had refused to

——— ✍ ———

Man's death is a result of God's judgment on their sin.

——— ✍ ———

believe that God could bring them into the Promised Land (Num. 32:10-15). Because of their sin of unbelief, God's anger burned against them. He therefore made them wander in the wilderness until they had all died. Moses admits this and says to God, "We have been consumed by Your anger, and by Your wrath we are terrified" (v. 7).

With great insight Moses says that man's death is a result of God's judgment on their sin. We might think that he would have compared the holiness of God with the sin of man here, just as he had compared the eternality of God with the brevity of man's life in the previous section. But instead he shows that the wages of sin is death. Every stop in the wilderness would have necessitated many burials. God's wrath against their sin had consumed them and terrified them. God set their iniquities before Him

(v. 8), the iniquities of rebellion, idolatry, and disobedience. Their sins included not only public ones but the hidden sins of grumbling and unbelief only seen by God. They were all naked and open in the light of God's presence. Thus the people were accountable to Him. New Testament believers are exhorted to allow God's Word to accomplish its purifying work in discerning the thoughts and intents of our hearts and revealing them clearly to us to aid in our sanctification (Heb. 4:11-13).

Man's Brief and Afflicted Life (vv. 9-10)

In verse 9 we learn the life of the Israelites in the wilderness was shortened because of God's justice and wrath toward them. Their years ended with a sigh, or whisper. Moses gives an average life span as seventy years, though he was much older than that himself. Around seventy or eighty years of age, many find life to be wearisome and sorrowful. In David's lifetime there was a man named Barzillai who commented on his eightieth birthday, "Can I discern between the good and bad? Can your servant taste what I eat or what I drink? Can I hear any longer the voice of singing men and singing women?" (2 Sam. 19:35). His life had become drudgery. Life for all of us "is soon cut off, and we fly away." Some old people boast about their age, but their functional losses and weakness are usually not easy to endure.

A Prayer for Wisdom (vv. 11-12)

Moses responds by praying to understand the meaning of our short lives on earth. He desires to react wisely in light of God's righteous wrath. He poses a rhetorical question. "Who knows the power of Your anger?" And the answer is that no one really understands the extent of the wrath of God. No one gives God the fear that is due to Him or responds in the reverence that befits Him. Moses had seen thousands of graves in the wilderness that reminded him of God's justice and His wrath against sin.

Many people do not want us to think like this. They suggest that we should only preach God's love, not His anger against sin. The truth is that we cannot exaggerate the extent of His wrath. Psalm 7:11 says that God is angry at sin every day, and the epistle to the Romans begins with the fact that "the wrath of God is revealed from heaven against all ungodliness and unrighteousness of men" (Rom. 1:18). It is therefore our duty to warn sinners to flee from the wrath to come (Mark 3:7).

In light of God's wrath and the brevity of our life, Moses prays, "So teach us to number our days, that we may gain a heart of wisdom" (v. 12). We are to seek God's instructions on the priorities of time because our days on earth are few. We should heed Scriptures like, "Seek first the kingdom of God and His righteousness" (Matt. 6:33). Applying that exhortation, we must choose whether we will participate in that activity, see that movie, or read that magazine. The point here is that God numbers our days, so we must invest them wisely. An old line of poetry reads, "Only one life, 'twill soon be past; only what's done for Christ will last." The prayer in verse 12 reveals a heartfelt desire to please God every day by the way we live. Paul counseled the Ephesian believers: "See then that you walk circumspectly, not as fools but as wise, redeeming the time, because the days are evil" (5:15-16). We should live with eternity's values in view.

> We should live with eternity's values in view.

A Prayer for God to Make Their Lives Joyful (vv. 13-15)

In the final section of this psalm, Moses prays for God's mercy. Notice the word "return" in verse 13. It is connected with what God says to us all at the conclusion of life (v. 3). He prays that God may return to them with compassion before the time comes when He returns them to destruction, or dust. The phrase, "How long?" asks how much longer they will be under God's discipline and how long it may be until His blessing returns. Moses goes on praying, "Oh, satisfy us early with Your mercy, that we may rejoice and be glad all our days!" (v. 14).

When we study the Psalms we must remember that they are written from man's perspective, and a Jewish one at that. The blessing that God had promised Israel was earth-bound. But even from the perspective of all human beings, it is natural to want our lives on earth to be free of adversity. This is the thrust of the desire expressed in verse 15. As New Testament believers, however, we should both thank God for trouble-free times and recognize God's love and mercy on a daily basis even in trials. This will bring joy that will truly satisfy our hearts and will not be dependent on circumstances. The New Testament perspective is that "our light affliction, which is but for a moment, is working for us a far more exceeding and eternal weight of glory" (2 Cor. 4:17). This is the eternal purpose of discipline and trials.

A Prayer for God to Fulfill His Purpose Through Them (v. 16)

Moses then prays, "Let Your work appear to Your servants, and Your glory to their children." God's "work" refers to the establishment of Israel in the Promised Land. He had been accomplishing this "work" ever since He announced it to Abraham (Gen. 15:13-16). The completion of this "work" with God's people in Canaan would put God's glory and splendor on display to their "children." The parents in the wilderness had failed and did not get to enjoy Canaan. But Moses prays that their children would go further than they had—that under Joshua's leadership they would trust God, see Him at work on their behalf in Canaan, and give Him the glory.

> We should exercise faith and enter into the realm of spiritual victory.

To apply this to our lives today, we don't have to be like the Israelites who were redeemed from Egypt but who, for lack of faith, never went on to enjoy spiritual victories and blessing. We who have been redeemed by Christ and indwelt by God's Spirit should exercise faith and enter into the realm of spiritual victory, pictured by the Israelites' final entrance into Canaan and victory over their enemies.

A Prayer for God to Make Their Lives Useful (v. 17)

In concluding his prayer, Moses says, "And let the beauty of the LORD our God be upon us." In verse 1 the name for God is "God" (Hebrew, Elohim), the Creator God. In verse 2 He is the LORD (Hebrew, Yahweh), the covenant God. But here in the final verse these two are combined and He is the "LORD our God," or "Yahweh our Elohim." It is the beauty or favor of God in all His fullness that Moses prays may be upon His people.

In the second part of the last verse Moses appeals to God to establish the work of the hands of His people. For the Israelites it was to go forward and enter the Land of Promise. For us, the work of our hands is to finish the work that He has given us to do in the time we have left (Phil. 2:13). It is good to know that God is able to establish, or confirm, our service for Him and thus bring blessing to others. Then His favor will be upon us, and the coming generation will not repeat the foolishness that we may have allowed.

10

PSALM 99
THE LORD IS MY RIGHTEOUS KING

Psalm 99 is the seventh of eight psalms that celebrate the King on the throne. They are called the "enthronement" psalms. Three of them begin with the declaration, "The LORD reigns" (Psalms 93, 97, and 99). That phrase occurs again in Psalm 96:10. All eight of them look forward to the establishment of the Davidic throne on earth that will be occupied by David's great descendant, the Messiah, the Lord Jesus Christ. They anticipate a time of great joy welcoming the holy King to His throne and enjoying His righteous rule.

Historical Background

The similarity of these eight psalms indicates that they have the same author, but he is nowhere named. Most modern commentators believe that these psalms were written in the 5th century BC to celebrate the return of the exiles from the Babylonian captivity. However, some of the oldest translations (such as the Septuagint) ascribe all eight of these psalms to David, that is, much earlier. This is supported by internal evidence from the reference to the existing Ark of the Covenant, which disappeared from the pages of Scripture about 605 BC. Thus the psalm seems to have been written prior to that. Our conclusion is that these eight enthronement psalms were probably written by King David in the 10th century BC.

Structure

The structure of Psalm 99 is sometimes viewed as having two sections: worship at God's footstool (vv. 1-5), and worship at God's holy hill (vv. 6-9). However, a more common way to structure the psalm is to divide it into three sections, each leading up to a climax of worship on the basis of God's holiness.

> ➤ Verses 1-3 end with "Let them praise Your great . . . name—He is holy."
> ➤ Verses 4-5 end with "And worship at His footstool—He is holy."
> ➤ Verses 6-9 end with "worship at His holy hill; for the LORD our God is holy."

God Is Holy

The focus of Psalm 99 is God's holiness, which is one of His chief attributes mentioned in Scripture. God's holiness is the only attribute that is emphasized by repeating it

————— ❧ —————
God's holiness is what sets Him apart from His creation.
————— ❧ —————

three times, as in Isaiah 6:3 and Revelation 4:8. In Hebrew, the repetition of a word signifies emphasis. Thus when the word "holy" is repeated three times as in this psalm, we must understand that it is significant. God's holiness is what sets Him apart from His creation. He is holy because He is separate from everything else in the universe. He is holy because He is above all created things in authority. He is holy because His moral righteousness stands alone far above every other act, word, or thought in the universe.

"The LORD Reigns" (vv. 1-3)

"Tremble!" (v. 1)

The first section of Psalm 99 begins with the declaration that "The LORD reigns," a favorite expression in the enthronement psalms (see Psalms 93 and 97). Many years before David, Moses recognized God's reign at the climax of his song of triumph after crossing the Red Sea. He said, "The LORD shall reign forever and ever" (Ex. 15:18). Hundreds of years later, Isaiah extolled the messenger who would proclaim the good news of salvation and say to Zion in the future, "Your God reigns!" (Isa. 52:7).

When the Son of God came to earth, however, and offered Himself to His people as their King, they rejected Him, saying, "We will not have this man to reign over us" (Luke 19:14). Nevertheless, in the last days, when the armies of Antichrist have been put down, all the angels and the redeemed in heaven will join in singing, "The Lord God Omnipotent reigns!" (Rev.

19:6). We too should acknowledge that God reigns, and when we do, it gives us encouragement to live for Him in this world stained by evil. It also gives us hope for the future time, when every enemy will be destroyed and He will reign forever and ever (Rev. 11:15).

In light of the fact that the Lord reigns, the psalmist advises, "Let the peoples tremble!" (v. 1). The peoples, or nations, should tremble with fear because they are accountable to Him and He will judge them. But today few (if any) nations or their leaders tremble in fear at the thought of God's majesty and rule. The imagery here is of Yahweh sitting on a throne in heaven receiving those who come to bow before Him in worship. His throne is placed between two cherubim, the angelic guardians of His throne. Ancient kings had royal guards standing on each side of their thrones.

Cherubim (high-ranking angels) were a distinctive part of the mercy seat, the covering for the Ark of the Covenant, which was the focal point of God's earthly dwelling (Ex. 25:17-22). The mercy seat and the cherubim were all fashioned from a single piece of gold. On it, the high priest sprinkled the blood of atonement (covering) once a year to make it possible for the nation to be acceptable to God. God's righteous wrath against sin was satisfied (propitiated) by that blood. The eyes of these two cherubim were focused on the mercy seat sprinkled with blood, the precise place where God's holy presence could meet sinful man (Ex. 25:20). God was therefore accessible to them on the basis of the sacrificial blood sprinkled there (Lev. 16:13-15).

"The LORD is great in Zion" (v. 2)

Verse 2 continues that the King will be called great and awesome in Zion and exalted above all the peoples (v. 2). Zion is essentially the city of Jerusalem. It was captured by David and became the political and spiritual center of Israel (2 Sam. 5:7). Israel honored its first king, Saul, because he was physically head and shoulders above all the people. How much more should we glory in our Lord Jesus Christ, whom God has highly exalted and to whom He has given a name that is above every name.

"Let them praise Your great and awesome name" (v. 3)

In light of the glory of His reign, David summons the peoples, to praise God's "great and awesome name." His name reflects His character. It is easy for believers to praise His great name when we think of God's love, grace, and faithfulness. It may not be so easy to praise Him when we think of His wrath in judgment. But the truth is that when our holy God acts in line with His holiness, it is always a time for praise.

This stanza concludes with the first of three affirmations that "He is holy." Isaiah's response to his vision of God's holiness was an overwhelming sense of his own lack of holiness, for he cried out, "Woe is me" (Isa. 6:5). Job too was persuaded of God's holiness and said, "I abhor myself, and repent in dust and ashes" (Job 42:6). The apostle Peter was confronted with the holiness of Jesus when he saw the great haul of fish, and he cried out, "I am a sinful man, O Lord!" (Luke 5:8). It is an awesome thing to confront the holiness of God.

The King Reigns Righteously (vv. 4-5)

The King Loves Justice (v. 4)

The second section of Psalm 99 deals with the Lord reigning over His people and the nations with righteousness. God's righteousness, or moral uprightness, is one of the elements of His holiness. Three things are said in verse 4 about the King's righteous rule. First, "The King's strength also loves justice." This means that in the strength of his political power and influence, David values God's moral standards and justice as his guiding rule. Human leaders with power and influence are very easily corrupted into thinking they have the right to compromise God's moral standards.

When David reached the pinnacle of his career as king of Israel it was said of him that he administered "judgment and justice" (1 Chron. 18:14). His army under Joab was defeating the Ammonites (2 Samuel 10). But one evening he saw Bathsheba, lusted after her, fell into moral sin with her, and then arranged for her husband's death (2 Samuel 11). Years later, David's son Solomon reached the pinnacle of his kingly career when the Queen of Sheba visited and praised God that Solomon had been made king "to do justice and righteousness" (1 Kings 10:9). But then the next chapter begins, "But King Solomon loved many foreign women" (1 Kings 11:1). Then *his* moral uprightness fell apart, and it was not long before his kingdom did as well. Human beings fail, both the ones in high places and the ordinary man on the street.

The second thing that marks the King's righteous rule in verse 4 is that He has established equity. In His kingdom there is no hypocrisy, no bias, no favoritism, no abuse of power. The third thing about His righteous rule in this verse is that He always does what is righteous. The emphasis is on the word "He" meaning that in contrast to human kings, He, the coming King, acts righteously. And the character of His kingdom reflects His own personal character. Our Sovereign is holy.

"Worship at His footstool" (v. 5)

David's conclusion in light of God the King's righteous rule is that we should "exalt the LORD our God, and worship at His footstool." In Isaiah 66:1, the earth is referred to as God's footstool. In Isaiah 60:13-14, Zion, the City of God is His footstool. And in 1 Chronicles 28:2, His footstool is the Ark of the Covenant. In our verse here, His footstool most likely refers to the Ark because of the reference to the cherubim that we noted in verse 1. The Ark was a chest kept in the Holy of Holies in the tabernacle. That place was so holy that it could only be approached once a year on the Day of Atonement, and then only by the High Priest. It contained the Ten Commandments of God's moral law that no person could fully keep. Thus, for all those who had broken the law it was a fearful place.

> "Exalt the LORD our God, and worship at His footstool."
> –Psalm 99:5

But the Ark was also a place of mercy, because the blood of an innocent sacrifice was sprinkled on its lid (the mercy seat). That blood was an atonement (covering) for man's sin so that he could approach God. The atoning blood of the goat on the Day of Atonement pointed to the blood of the Lord Jesus Christ by which we are saved. And because God's anger against sin has been righteously satisfied we can "exalt the LORD our God, and worship at His footstool."

When we worship at His footstool we are symbolically bowing at His feet in humility. We are to be like Mary of Bethany, who anointed the feet of Jesus with fragrant oil and wiped them with her hair (John 11:2, 12:3). Like her we are to exalt our Savior by bowing low before Him. True worship is when we submit to God's sovereignty as our King and to His grace as our Redeemer. The second stanza ends as the first one did with a reminder that "He is holy" (v. 5).

"The LORD our God is Holy" (vv. 6-9)

Three Godly Leaders (vv. 6-7)

In the final stanza the psalmist changes his focus. Here he points us to three godly leaders on earth who responded to God as their King. They are Moses, Aaron, and Samuel. Moses and Aaron were "among His priests." Moses performed priestly duties and appointed Aaron as the first official high priest of Israel (Ex. 24:6-8, 28:1). Samuel was a prophet, but he too exercised some priestly duties when the priesthood of Eli failed (1 Sam. 3:20, 7:10). Samuel's father, Elkanah, came from a priestly line.

The point that the psalmist makes is that all three of these men were intercessors, that is, men of prayer. In the circumstances surrounding each of them, the nation had insulted the holiness of God by its disobedience and was subsequently under judgment. These three men interceded on behalf of sinful Israel. They prayed for God's mercy and He granted their request to withhold further judgment.

Moses prayed for his people when they made the golden calf and worshipped it instead of God (Ex. 32:11-14). Aaron prayed when Korah led a rebellion and tried to usurp the priesthood (Num. 16:41-50). And Samuel prayed for God's mercy after King Saul and his army disobeyed God's command to utterly destroy the Amalekites (1 Sam. 15:9-11). All three of these men called upon God to withhold judgment, and He answered them.

These three men of prayer not only spoke to God, but they also heard God speak to them. Verse 7 says that, "He spoke to them in the cloudy pillar," referring to the same pillar of cloud that God used to lead the Israelites out of Egypt. Later God spoke to them from that cloud when it rested on Mount Sinai, and then above the tabernacle (Ex. 13:21, 24:15, 40:34). Moses and Aaron had both seen the cloud and heard God speak from it in the wilderness. Samuel did not see the pillar of cloud, but he certainly heard God's voice from the tabernacle (1 Samuel 3). Having heard God speak, "They kept His testimonies and the ordinance He gave them" (v. 7b). That is, they obeyed God. The point is that when the Israelites rebelled against God, Moses, Aaron, and Samuel remained faithful to Him and true to His precepts. They had an open ear to hear God's voice, an open eye to see the evidence of God's presence, and a willing heart to obey God's command.

The King Judges and Disciplines Righteously (v. 8)

The prayers of these three righteous men were effective, for the God of the covenant answered them and forgave the nation. The nation was spared from His full wrath. But in His wisdom God still disciplined them and "took vengeance on their deeds." That is, He reminded them by His discipline to take His holiness seriously. In the case of the sin of worshiping the golden calf, although Moses prayed and the nation was spared, God commanded those who were, like Him, offended by this rebellion, to judge his neighbor. In response to that challenge, the men of the tribe of Levi slaughtered 3,000 Israelites that day (Ex. 32:26-28).

In the case of the rebellion of Korah, the earth swallowed up Korah and fire consumed 250 others who offered incense. When the people still murmured against God, Aaron prayed for God's mercy as he waved the censer between the living and the dead. But in a disciplinary measure, God killed 14,700 more people in a plague (Num. 16:32-35, 49). Our holy God is a consuming fire.

In the third example, King Saul had flouted the commandment of God and spared the Ammonite king as well as the livestock. Samuel prayed for them and God spared the nation, yet He rejected King Saul and anointed David to be king in his place (1 Samuel 15). In all three cases God saved the nation in His mercy but disciplined them in His holiness. And for His people today, God saves us by His grace, but He disciplines us "for our profit" and to conform us to the image of His Son (Rom. 8:28-29; Heb. 12:5-11). We should respond to such discipline with humility and a yielded spirit, recognizing that God seeks to mature us through it, not punish us (Heb. 12:11).

"Exalt the LORD our God" (v. 9)

The third stanza has given us the examples of God's dealings with the nation led by Moses, Aaron, and Samuel. Now it closes with the command that we should exalt God and worship at His holy hill. His holy hill was the temple mount in Jerusalem where the tabernacle stood, and later, the temple (Ps. 15:1, 24:3). It was the place of worship that symbolized God's presence with them.

What is important is our attitude toward God in worship.

In John 4:24 the Lord Jesus told the woman at the well that "God is Spirit" and that what is important is our attitude toward God in worship, not attendance at a particular location. Praise the Lord, we can come into His presence anywhere and at any time and worship Him in spirit and in truth. And when we do, we can join the Old Testament believers in exalting the Lord our God, for He is holy.

11

PSALM 103
THE LORD IS MY GRACIOUS
BENEFACTOR

Psalm 103 is a favorite of God's people because it beautifully expresses the praise and thanks they would like to offer God. A well loved hymn, "Praise, my soul, the king of heaven" is based on it. In this psalm, David's praise expands in ever-widening circles. In the first five verses he speaks to his own soul to awaken it to worship. In verses 6 to 18 he widens the scope of his exhortation to include God's earthly people.

> *Forgetfulness is often the source of ingratitude.*

Then he addresses the much larger audience of God's angelic hosts, calling on them to add their voices to the chorus of those who bless the Lord (vv. 20-21). Finally, he calls on all the works of creation in the entire universe to join in blessing God (v. 22).

A Call to Praise the Lord for Personal Blessings (vv. 1-5)

"Bless the LORD, O my soul" (vv. 1-2)

David was a man very attuned to appreciating God's sovereign majesty and the wonders of everything God does. In light of this, David exhorts his soul to remember all the benefits that God had showered on him and to never forget them. The *soul* of a person as David uses the word here is the essence of his person, his inner being as distinct from his body. It consists of his thinking and emotions. Forgetfulness is often the source of ingratitude, so David calls on *all* of his being to remember *all* the Lord's benefits. Memory is a treacherous thing. It tends to recall details of trials and forgets the good things. It is even more treacherous when it remembers the hard times as "bad" rather than as God's gracious dealings that are for our spiritual maturity.

To "bless the Lord" is to glorify and honor Him with a thankful heart in response to His gracious dealings with us. There ought to never be a time when we cannot bless God, because everything He does is consistent with His holy character. It is a good idea to do as the classic hymn exhorts: "Count your blessings, name them one by one." And that is exactly what the psalmist does here. He counsels his soul to name God's blessings one by one. The "who" is repeated five times to emphasize that each benefit comes from the Lord.

"Who forgives all your iniquities" (v. 3)

Forgiveness of sins is the first and most important of all God's benefits we enjoy if we are one of His redeemed people. As New Testament believers, we look back on the reason God can forgive us—on the basis of His Son's redeeming blood (Eph. 1:7). God justifies us because the full price of our sin has been paid for by Christ. The assurance of

> Forgiveness is a current, ongoing spiritual blessing that we should continually relish.

sins forgiven that David enjoyed was on the basis of blood offerings he would have made in faith, according to the sacrificial system God had ordained for Israel. Notice, however, that David speaks in the present tense. Forgiveness is a current, ongoing spiritual blessing that we should continually relish; it is not just relevant to our eternal state to do with our justification. God continues to forgive us in a family, relational sense because we still commit sins every day. Since this psalm was probably written late in David's life, he would have been especially aware of God's forgiveness for his sins of adultery and murder.

"Who heals all your diseases"

The word "diseases" is the parallel word to iniquities and should be understood in a moral sense. David was not speaking of physical ailments here. In this passage, just as in Isaiah 53, we are told that "He [Christ] was bruised for our iniquities. . . . And by His stripes we are healed." True believers are immediately healed from the moral disease of sin when they put their faith in Christ for the salvation of their souls.

"Who redeems your life from destruction" (v. 4)

"Destruction" is a reference to the grave (Sheol), as in Psalm 16:10. God redeemed His people Israel from slavery in Egypt (Deut. 7:8; 13:5). David did not have complete understanding of redemption as he lived before Christ came, but he understood the deliverance that God brought about for ancient Israel in Egypt. It pictures the redeeming grace of God that releases those who believe in Christ from the bondage of sin. "Christ has redeemed us from the curse of the law, having become a curse for us" (Gal. 3:13).

"Who crowns you with loving-kindness"

David rejoices that God had crowned his life with mercies. God had preserved David through many narrow escapes so that he could be king. Think of the jaw of the lion, the paw of the bear, the sword of Goliath, the betrayal of the men of Keilah, the pursuit of King Saul, and the rebellion of his own son Absalom. These were God's mercies to David, and out of them he became and remained king. The imagery of the crown in this passage is not of earning it by winning a race; it is a crown of mercy, not of merit.

"Who satisfies your mouth with good things" (v. 5)

David continues to address his own soul. Verse 5 literally means "filling with good your soul." God does not give us everything we might desire, but He gives us everything in harmony with His goodness.

When David's soul responds to these named benefits by blessing God, then his "youth is renewed like the eagle's." The eagle is a symbol of the youth and strength that is spiritually renewed in the believer as he or she waits on the Lord and blesses Him for His benefits (Isa. 40:31). Contrast this with Psalm 102:6, where the psalmist sits dejected and lonely like the owl of the desert and like the sparrow on the housetop. Here in Psalm 103 he rises like the eagle to ever-increasing heights. Thus when our souls are blessing (praising) the Lord in thankfulness because He forgives, heals, redeems, crowns, and satisfies us, our spirits soar in the spiritual heavenlies.

A Call to Praise the Lord
for Corporate Blessings (vv. 6-10)

In the second section of Psalm 103, David exhorts his people to bless God for their national benefits in light of God's mercy and grace to them as a nation.

God's Righteousness and Justice (v. 6)

Israel was God's covenant people and should be aware of the righteous deeds and judgments of God as displayed in her own history (v. 6). When others oppressed them, God treated them with righteousness and justice (v. 6). David illustrates this by reminding them of their national history at the commencement of their wilderness journey from Egypt to Canaan under Moses' leadership. The Egyptians oppressed them, but God heard and responded to their cries. God showed His justice by punishing the Egyptians for enslaving His people. He did this by bringing plagues on the Egyptians—by killing all their firstborn and by drowning Pharaoh's army at the Red Sea. In these ways, God's grace abounded to Moses and to the whole nation.

God's Ways and Deeds (v. 7)

When Moses was alone with God on the mountain, he asked Him, "If I have found grace in Your sight, show me now Your way, that I may know You" (Ex. 33:12). Moses wanted to know more of the Lord's mercy, love, and forgiveness, because these attributes indicated the Lord's character. God made known His ways to Moses by revelation. He gave him the instructions concerning the law, the tabernacle, and the priesthood that illustrated His ways of grace and the delight of His presence.

The general population of Israel understood much less of God's gracious ways than Moses did. They saw God's mighty acts in opening a way through the Red Sea, in providing them with manna every morning, and in guiding them with the pillar of cloud and fire. And at Mount Sinai they witnessed God's acts in such things as the thunder and lightning, the terrifying voice of the Lord, and the burning cloud on the mountain. But their behavior at the bottom of the mountain (when they worshiped the golden calf) shows that they did not really appreciate how God's acts reflected His holy standards.

God's Mercy and Grace (vv. 8-10)

David goes on to quote from God's proclamation to Moses when the broken covenant was renewed at Mount Sinai: "The LORD, the LORD God, merciful and gracious, longsuffering, and abounding in goodness and truth, keeping mercy for thousands" (Ex. 34:6-7). No less than six of God's tremendous attributes are contained in this verse.

Verses 9 and 10 reflect in practice God's attributes of grace and mercy to His own people. His discipline is only ever a temporary measure. We see His grace illustrated in the period of exile set for the nation of Judah. God told them through His prophets that it would last for seventy years, and at the end of that period He did indeed sovereignly arrange their return to the Promised Land. This is an example to all of us not to hold grudges. God always offers pardon and works toward reconciliation with those who offend Him.

God's punishment is less than we deserve.

God's punishment is less then we deserve. In this He demonstrates His mercy. He does not judge our sins and iniquities by giving us what we deserve—if He did, we would be consigned to hell! We can therefore praise Him for what He has *not* done as well as for what He *has* done. His own Son has already borne the wrath we deserved.

Mercy as High as the Heavens (v. 11)

David describes the wonders of God's mercy and grace by comparing them to things we can understand. The psalmist borrows language from astronomy, geography, and parental love to describe them.

God abounds in mercy.

We learned in verse 8 that God abounds in mercy. His mercy is so vast it can only be described by astronomical terms—it is compared to the height of the heavens above the earth. Today we talk of the distance between earth and the stars and galaxies in terms of thousands of light years, but even astronomers have not yet discovered any end to the universe. So great is God's mercy toward those who fear Him.

Grace as Wide as East is from West (v. 12)

When a person trusts in the living God for the salvation of their soul, their sins are said to be removed as far as the east is from the west. Neither

> ❧
>
> **Jesus has borne our sins away an infinite distance.**
>
> ❧

east nor west has a terminal point on earth, unlike north and south. Thus, the distance from east to west is not measurable, because on a spherical earth both continue without either a starting point or terminus. Jesus, as our scapegoat, has borne our sins away an infinite distance. Infinity therefore represents how far His mercy has removed our transgressions from us.

Compassion as Great as a Father's (vv. 13-14)

God's loving-kindness is likened to the compassion of a father for his son. The father knows his son, including all his weaknesses and strengths. But his love will go to any lengths for the son's benefit. Our heavenly Father knows our physical frame and how we were formed in the beginning. He remembers that He fashioned the first man from dust as part of His creation. He made man into a living soul (Gen. 2:7) who will return to dust (Gen. 3:19, Ps. 90:3). Although man is only dust, God set His love on him. When a believer sins, God deals with him in mercy that flows from His compassion. "So the LORD pities [has compassion on] those who fear Him."

Responding to God's Eternal Mercies (vv. 15-18)

God's loving-kindness and righteousness are eternal compared to the mortality of man. The phrase "as for man" refers to man in his weakness and frailty. Human life is so short that it is compared to that of grass. It grows, matures, dies, and is gone within a few short months. It is good for us to see the brevity of our lives on earth in these terms (vv. 15-17; cf. Isa. 40:6-12). The wind referred to here is the gentle wind that causes the petals to drop and the flowers to disappear. It is like people who reach the end of their lives and then pass into eternity. After a time, they are forgotten. Quoting from Job 7:10, David says, "Its place remembers it no more." In time, the very place where men and women were well known and had great influence will not even remember their names.

In contrast to the brevity of human life, the psalmist proclaims that the loving-kindness of the Lord is everlasting (v. 18). It never fades or disappears because it reflects His eternal person (Ps. 102:27). His perpetual mercy follows the righteous, who are broadly characterized here as those who fear Him, who keep His covenant, and who remember His commandments all the days of their lives (v. 18). And beyond that, God's righteousness continues on down the family line of the godly to their children and grandchildren. Godly parents respond to God's mercy by intentionally having effectual spiritual influence on succeeding generations (cf. Ex. 20:6).

A Call to Praise the Lord
for Universal Blessings (vv. 19-21)

"The LORD has established His throne" (v. 19)

The concept of God's universal sovereignty introduces a call to the whole universe. The Lord has established His throne in heaven, from which He rules everything. Conditions there are sublime and eternal. He is surrounded there by a worshipful crowd who join in praising Him. The apostle John, in his vision, saw the great multitude in heaven shouting God's praise like the sound of many waters, "Alleluia! Salvation and glory and honor and power belong to the Lord our God! . . . Alleluia! For the Lord God Omnipotent reigns!" (Rev. 19:1, 6). Thus the psalmist reminds us here that God's throne is established and His kingdom reigns over all (v. 19).

"Bless the LORD, you His angels" (v. 20)

David now brings the theme of blessing the Lord to a climax (vv. 20-22). It is sometimes called the "The Song of the Three Children."

First he calls on the mighty angels around God's throne to bless the Lord (v. 20). They excel in strength for their work of guarding people, cities, and nations. In later Jewish history, when the Assyrian army surrounded Jerusalem in the days of Hezekiah, one angel destroyed 185,000 soldiers in a single night (2 Kings 19:35). When Daniel's three friends were in the burning fiery furnace, an angel delivered them (Dan. 3:28). Angels heed God's voice. So David calls on them to "bless the LORD."

"Bless the Lord, all you His hosts" (v. 21)

Second, David calls on the hosts of heaven to bless the Lord (v. 21). The "hosts" probably refer to the sun, the moon, the planets, and the stars. These heavenly bodies "do His pleasure." They stay in the orbits He designed for them. They do His will. The sun gives us heat and light. The moon illumines the night. The stars guide us in travel, and their names declare God's glory (Ps. 19:1). The stars are often associated with angels in the Old Testament Scriptures (Job 38:7).

"Bless the Lord, all His works" (v. 22)

Third, he calls on all God's created works to worship Him (v. 22). Psalm 145:10 echoes this theme with "All Your works shall praise You, O Lord." And in Psalm 148:7-13 the theme resounds again. "Praise the Lord from the earth, you great sea creatures and all the depths; fire and hail, snow and clouds; stormy wind, fulfilling His word; mountains and all hills; fruitful trees and all cedars. . . . Let them praise the name of the Lord, for His name alone is exalted" (Ps. 148:7-13).

Thus the angels, the heavenly bodies, and all created things are to bless the Lord with their praises. Since none of these can ever exhaust their praises, we should never let our souls forget to praise His glorious name. The psalm ends as it began, with the psalmist calling on his own soul to bless his God.

12

PSALM 139
THE LORD IS MY OMNISCIENT CREATOR

Psalm 139 is undoubtedly one of the best-loved psalms because it deals with the precious truth that the infinite God is intensely interested and involved in finite man, His prime creation. Our souls can be enriched when we embrace this truth. The psalm focuses on three of God's non-communicative attributes (ones that man cannot reflect in any way): His omniscience, His omnipresence, and His omnipotence. These mean that God is all-knowing, always present, and all-powerful, respectively. The psalmist does not write of these attributes abstractly as a theologian might, but in terms of how they affect his relationship to God; he does not therefore use the language of theologians, but the lyrics of a poet. His main theme is that God, in His omniscience, knows everything about him personally. God's infinite knowledge of us is substantiated by His universal presence and by His unlimited power. This psalm is not written for our head knowledge, but for our heart: it conveys the need we have for a personal God who is interested in us personally. Take note of the numerous singular personal pronouns: "I," "me," and "my."

> **Psalm 139 is not written for our head knowledge, but for our heart.**

It is a remarkable thing that God wants to have personal relationship with us, His creatures. The depth of that relationship depends on how we respond to His knowledge of us. This psalm helps us understand all that God knows about our strengths and weaknesses, our successes and failures, our sins and our graces. When we grasp that we cannot hide anything from Him, we come to Him in confession and humility, dealing with each barrier that stands between Him and ourselves. As these barriers come down, our relationship with Him deepens into true fellowship.

Structure

The title of the psalm tells us that David wrote it "for the chief musician at the tabernacle." It was this man's responsibility to put these words to music so that instruments and voices could join in corporate worship. When the people brought their offerings to the altar they could listen to the choir of Levites singing these psalms. We too can profit from these lyrics.

The psalm has four easily recognizable sections of six verses each. In the first three sections David describes God's omniscience (vv. 1-6), omnipresence (vv. 7-12), and omnipotence (vv. 13-18) respectively. We have noted that the first of these is the overall theme of the psalm. David includes the other two attributes to further explain God's omniscience. God knows everything because He is everywhere at the same time and because He made everything that exists. The fourth section (vv. 19-24) is David's personal response to God's intimate knowledge of him.

God's Omniscience (vv. 1-6)

> God discerns what is good and bad in us as He follows our course during the day.

David begins in verse 1 with his thesis that God knows him through and through. He confesses, "O Lᴏʀᴅ, You have searched me and known me." The second "me" is not in the original text, so the emphasis is on God's *knowing,* not "me," the object of His knowing. It reflects David's wonder and amazement that God saw and knew everything about him. The word "search" is a mining term, conveying the idea of searching and digging for precious metals (cf. Job 28:3). We must not press this thought too far because God does not have to search for the unknown—He already knows everything. In poetic language, the point here is that, from David's viewpoint, God knows every personal detail about us as thoroughly as a miner knows the geological details of the area where gold is found.

David expands on this theme in verses 2 to 4. As well as knowing David's day-to-day movements, God even knows his thoughts "afar off," that is, before they were even formulated in his mind (v. 2). The idea of God "comprehending his path" is thought to connect to winnowing, the process that separates grain from chaff. Thus, God discerns what is good and bad in us as He follows our course during the day. He knows the hidden motives behind every action and every thought. God knows every single word our tongues have ever formed. Some translations have it, "even before there was a word on my tongue" (v. 4).

The phrase about God's hedging David in is best understood as God hedging him in to protect him rather than restricting his movements. It reminds us of when Satan complained to God about Job, "Have You not made a hedge around him?" (Job 1:10). David is reflecting that God knew the dangers around him and thus He enclosed David in His protective care by watching out for him, just as a mother watches out for her children playing in the street. David goes on to say that God guides him with His hand upon him. A good illustration is that of a human father teaching his little son to ride a two-wheel bike. He positions himself behind the boy, watching the way ahead with his hand on his back to steady him.

In light of all that God knows about him, David exclaims, "Such knowledge is too wonderful for me; it is high, I cannot attain it." This kind of response to God's knowledge is an exclamation of worship. David realizes that it is beyond his ability to even imagine all that God knows about him. Rather than try to grasp something that seems incomprehensible to us, all we should do at that point is worship Him.

God's Omnipresence (vv. 7-12)

In verse 7, David's thought processes about God's complete personal knowledge of him lead him to pose two questions: "Where can I go from Your Spirit? Or where can I flee from Your presence?" It's not that David *wants* to escape from God's presence, as the answer is obviously "nowhere." It is in fact a great comfort to David that God is present wherever he goes.

David meditates on this grand concept and considers three extreme realms in the universe to emphasize God's omnipresence, again posing rhetorical questions. First, God inhabits both heaven and the grave. Hell in the Hebrew is "sheol," the place of the dead. The prophet Amos uses similar language in describing people who foolishly think that they can escape God's judgment. "Though they dig into hell, from there My hand shall take them; though they climb up to heaven, from there I will bring them down" (Amos 9:2).

Second, God inhabits the whole earth. The "wings of the morning" refer to the rays fanning out from the rising sun in the east. The sea refers to the Mediterranean Sea, which lies west of the land of Israel. The prophet Jonah tried to escape from God by taking a ship westward from Joppa to Tarshish (on the coast of what is Spain today). But God sent a storm to cause Jonah to be tossed overboard and then sent a great fish to swallow Jonah. There in the belly of the fish God met Jonah. There was no escape. From the wings of the dawn in the east to the belly of the great fish in the west, God was there.

David comments, "Even there Your hand shall lead me, and Your right hand shall hold me" (v. 10). God's right hand refers to His power, as Moses said when God opened a way for the Israelites through the Red Sea. His words were, "Your right hand, O Lord, has become glorious in power" (Ex. 15:6). It is the same right hand that stretched out the heavens in creation (Isa. 48:13).

God is also in the darkness. Many wicked people today choose to do their evil deeds under cover of darkness. But there is nowhere to hide from God in the dark. Darkness may hide men from men, but it does not hide anyone from God. Light and darkness are the same to Him.

God's Omnipotence (vv. 13-18)

The Marvel of God's Creation of David (vv. 13-16)

David began the psalm with the theme of God's omniscience (vv. 1-6). He then explains God's universal knowledge with the fact that He is universally present (vv. 7-12). God knows David because He is with David everywhere. In this section, David further illustrates God's supreme knowledge with the truth that He is supremely powerful. The example he uses to illustrate God's power is his own physical birth—an apt example, given the personal nature and tone of the whole psalm. God knows David because He made David's human body, soul, and spirit. God made *everything* that exists and He controls it with His supreme power (vv. 13-18).

David says, in effect, "No wonder God knows me—He made me. He oversaw every detail of my being from the moment of conception in the workshop of my mother's womb." The term translated "inward parts" in verse 13 is the Hebrew word for kidneys. The kidneys were understood by ancients to be the seat of human emotions and moral character (cf. Ps. 26:2, 7:9). The word "covered" is the Hebrew word for woven and refers to the interweaving of bones, sinews, and muscles in the developing baby. Thus these two phrases in verse 13 refer to God's oversight in both the emotional and physical formation of every detail of the child in the womb.

It is not surprising that David now exclaims, "I will praise You, for I am fearfully and wonderfully made" (v. 14). Today we might say, "Your deeds are awesome and amazing." For at the moment of the formation of the first cell at his conception, God programmed David's DNA with all its thousands of elements to become the individual He designed David to be. So David continues, "Marvelous are Your works, and that my soul knows very well. My frame was not hidden from You, when I was made in secret."

Even when David was an unformed embryo, the omniscient God knew every feature of his anatomy. David said, I was "skillfully wrought [embroidered in a beautiful design by a skilled artisan] in the lowest parts of the earth" (v. 15). The phrase "lowest parts of the earth" parallels the phrase "in secret" in the same verse. Both phrases poetically refer to the womb of the mother in which every child has been skillfully wrought by God according to the design He has planned.

A thoughtful study of the human body ought to cause us to wonder in awe at the design of its bones, muscles, and blood vessels. But even that is only a tiny part of the chemical, electrical, and neurological systems. Some further knowledge of the mind-boggling complexity of microbiology should cause us to fall down and worship at the feet of our all-knowing, all-powerful God. What a revelation this psalm contains concerning the sanctity and dignity of the unborn child! And all that design was programmed into the very first cell formed at conception. This is an important passage for a biblical understanding of the facts that relate to the abortion issue.

God's intentions for David were all decided beforehand and recorded in His "book." An architect lays out his plans with a list of specifications for the building he has in mind. In the same way, God the divine Architect set out His plans for us, His people, before we were born. These included His plans for each day of our lives (v. 16).

The Magnitude of God's Interest in David (vv. 17-18)

David's own formation was not a matter of chance; rather, God was directly involved in every stage of the process. David finds it extremely difficult to grasp the fact that Almighty God has given such particular attention to the innumerable details—in fact, every detail—of his own formation and life. This is the concept behind verse 17, as the word "precious" here means difficult, not valuable. The second half of verse 18 is difficult to interpret as it stands, as waking up from sleep does not seem to have anything to do with the context. The NET Bible translates this portion, "Even if I finished counting them [Your thoughts about me], I would still have to contend with You." The implication is that they are too innumerable to count.

David's Response to God (vv. 19-24)

"Judge the Wicked!" (vv. 19-22)

The psalm has thus far reflected David's appreciation of God's perfect knowledge and care of him. Now suddenly David's tone changes as he prays that God would pour out judgment on His enemies. Some commentators believe this change indicates that the temple musicians added this section later, perhaps when Jerusalem was under attack. But this can hardly be the case, because the beginning and the ending of the psalm both deal with God searching and knowing David. In the beginning he acknowledged the fact that God had searched him (v. 1). At the end, David prays that God would search his heart (vv. 23-24). This indicates unity in the psalm.

David's sudden prayer for God to judge the wicked is consistent with the theme of God's perfect knowledge. God is, after all, the Judge of all the earth, and because He does have complete knowledge about the evil of those who rebel against Him, He must judge them according to that knowledge. The ungodly are described in these verses as "wicked" and "bloodthirsty." They are guilty of blasphemy when they speak wickedly and take God's name in vain. They are the enemies of God and the enemies of God's people.

David, as one of the righteous, longs for evil in the world to be eradicated. It is not surprising therefore that he expects God to fulfill His role as Judge. He prays, "Oh, that You would slay the wicked, O God!" (v.

19). In praying that way he is not venting personal feelings; he is asking the all-knowing God to act righteously and consistently with His holiness. The omniscient God who sees all evil must surely judge all evil. David hates sin and is rightly indignant.

Many of us get so accustomed to the sin around us that we become overly tolerant. But those who reject the redemption that Christ gained for them by His work on Calvary will have to bear their own judgment. Our modern society tries to eliminate evil without dealing with the evildoers. It is with this principle in view that David says, "I . . . hate them . . . who hate You. . . . I count them my enemies" (vv. 20-21). We, like David, should strive to keep ourselves untainted by the evil around us. The difficulty for most of us is to separate our personal feelings from truly righteous indignation.

> We, like David, should strive to keep ourselves untainted by the evil around us.

"Judge me!" (vv. 23-24)

David's prayer in the last two verses is that God would search his own heart for any wickedness that might be found there. He has voiced sympathy for the holy judgment of God on sinners and he does not exclude himself. He asks that the all-seeing eye of God might examine him closely. It takes humility to submit to God by asking Him to search our hearts and in yielding to His assessment. "Try me and know my anxieties [misgivings]." These anxieties are those things that challenge our faith and lead us into sin. David wanted any sinful motives of his heart or sinful thoughts of his mind to be brought to light (John 3:21). Then he would gladly confess and forsake them. David wanted much more than to be able to identify his sins; he wanted to be corrected and restored. He wanted nothing less than to be conformed to God's will for him.

David acknowledges in the last verse that there are two ways, the "wicked way" and the "way everlasting" (v. 24). The first is the way of the world under God's judgment; the other is the way of holiness that leads to life and fellowship with God and which lasts into eternity. This verse reminds us of Psalm 1:6 that we studied at the beginning of this course: "For the Lord knows the way of the righteous, but the way of the ungodly shall perish." It is the way home to our Father-Creator. Those on this path live with the knowledge of God's omniscience and they rejoice in it as an ever-present comfort and strength. Those on the "wicked way" must also be aware of God's omniscience, but they should tremble in fear that they face the sure and certain judgment of God who knows every act, word, and thought of their lives.